What people are saying about …

LITTLE BLACK
SHEEP

"Every book I have written and each and every major undertaking in my ministry has been accompanied by the musical lyricism, passion, and perspicuity of Ashley Cleveland. There is a kind of gospel for those who know little of the jagged, haunting edge of the margins. And there is the same but different taste of the gospel for those who know the dark shadows, grandiose dreams, and squalor of self-incriminating sabotage. This gospel is not merely true but also wantonly excessive and unexpectedly beautiful. In my brokenness, I need a jagged and extravagant gospel, and this rare, stunningly beautiful, and broken woman sings what I suspect is the truest gospel I have ever heard. This book, like her music, delivers me face-to-face with a God who just might be good news. To say that I enjoyed the book is far from the truth. I devoured it. Wept. Raged. Swore. And said yes again to Jesus."

Dan B. Allender, PhD, professor of Counseling
Psychology and founding president of the
Seattle School of Theology and Psychology

"Ashley Cleveland is one of my favorite singer-songwriters. Her life and music are deeply rooted in her faith and nurtured by the love of God. In *Little Black Sheep*, she honestly shares her own human vulnerabilities and joyfully offers her amazing gifts. Ashley's music is always moving, and her story is deeply inspiring. Ashley's hymn singing has been church for me on many Sundays! In script and song, Ashley shows us how God works in one life at a time and through us to the whole world. Don't miss this."

Jim Wallis, president of Sojourners

"I had barely started the first chapter of *Little Black Sheep*, and I already knew that the lump in my throat and the teary laughter that oddly accompanied it would be with me for the entire read. They were. I laughed and cried the whole way through, so grateful for Ashley's honesty and for God's hold on her. I'm glad we are family. And for what it's worth, Ashley spoke a lot of truth into my life during those rag-legged years before her sobriety. Thank you, Ashley, for writing all of this down. Your narrative voice is compelling, and your story begs for the answer we are all asking: can we be loved … and if so, will we be changed by it?"

Amy Grant, singer and songwriter

"Ashley Cleveland—singer of sensitive, honest songs—has a way with words, and the plain story of sin and mercy she tells here is hauntingly powerful. Some readers will undoubtedly find her to be broken bread for their starving souls."

J. I. Packer, author of *Knowing God*

"Funny, smart, tender, honest—Ashley's memoir, *Little Black Sheep*, is a wonderful story of redemption. It will fill your heart with hope."

Sally Lloyd-Jones, author of the bestselling
and Christian Book Award-winning
Thoughts to Make Your Heart Sing

"*Little Black Sheep* is a remarkable story of redemption that Ashley tells with both honesty and reverence. It is neither neat nor tidy, but it is altogether hopeful. Through her brilliantly crafted memoir, you will be entertained, you will discover shades of your own story, and ultimately, you will find yourself drawn to the Savior who was with her the whole way."

Kelly Minter, author of the Bible study
Nehemiah and *The Fitting Room*

"Though it is an autobiography, *Little Black Sheep* is not really about my friend Ashley in the end. It is not about her life as much as it is about the One who gave her life and redeemed its brokenness. That she could tell such a complete and compelling story in so few pages is a testimony to a gifted writer."

Michael Card, Bible teacher, songwriter, and author of
A Sacred Sorrow and The Biblical Imagination Series

"*Little Black Sheep* roars with a powerful message of redemption that will grip your heart and keep you captivated from cover to cover. With a voice as strong on the page as on the stage, Ashley Cleveland unveils a complex and compelling life filled with triumph and fear, accolades and addictions, and the true compassion of a heavenly Father who saw her through it all."

Matt Bronleewe, award-winning songwriter, producer, and author

"*Little Black Sheep* is one of the bravest, most brutally honest, and most soul-inspiring books I have ever read. Ashley's story of her battle with addiction and her traumatic childhood is both fascinating and an absolute page-turner. Her willingness to lay out her brokenness in plain sight left me awestruck. Awe. Struck. As soon as I finished it, I wiped away tears and turned back to the first page so I could read it again. Beautiful, broken, and brilliant."

Cindy Morgan, singer and songwriter

"Little Black Sheep was hard to put down. It made me laugh out loud, cry, and drew me closer to Ashley as a fellow sojourner—and to God for His mercy and undeniable involvement in Ashley's life. This fast-paced and vulnerable tale of a wide-open life pulls no punches. It was worth every minute I spent reading it!"

Bruce Carroll, Grammy and Dove Award–
winning singer, songwriter, and worship leader

"Ashley Cleveland is one of the most authentic humans we have had the privilege of getting to know in over two decades of touring and recording. Her soulfulness shines through on every page of this wonderful memoir."

Linford Detweiler and **Karin Bergquist** of Over the Rhine

"I suppose there is a little black sheep in all of us. As she does with her music, Ashley Cleveland confronts us with her honesty and pain so deeply that we cannot help but face ourselves. But she does this in such a soft and tender way in her memoir that it will leave all of us nudged toward change. Let this book do some work on you."

Terry D. Hargrave, PhD, professor of Marriage
and Family Therapy at Fuller Theological
Seminary and author of *Forgiving the Devil*

LITTLE BLACK SHEEP

LITTLE BLACK SHEEP

A MEMOIR

ASHLEY CLEVELAND

David C Cook®
transforming lives together

LITTLE BLACK SHEEP
Published by David C Cook
4050 Lee Vance View
Colorado Springs, CO 80918 U.S.A.

David C Cook Distribution Canada
55 Woodslee Avenue, Paris, Ontario, Canada N3L 3E5

David C Cook U.K., Kingsway Communications
Eastbourne, East Sussex BN23 6NT, England

The graphic circle C logo is a registered trademark of David C Cook.

All Scripture quotations, unless otherwise indicated, are take
from the New King James Version®. Copyright © 1982 by Thomas
Nelson, Inc. Used by permission. All rights reserved.

LCCN 2013937517
ISBN 978-1-4347-0529-7
eISBN 978-0-7814-1087-8

The Team: Don Pape, John Blase, Nick Lee, Tonya Osterhouse, Karen Athen
Cover Design: Amy Konyndyk
Cover Painting: DL Taylor

Printed in the United States of America
First Edition 2013

1 2 3 4 5 6 7 8 9 10

061713

For Becca

CONTENTS

ACKNOWLEDGMENTS

Years ago my husband, Kenny, began suggesting that I write a book. Every time he brought it up, I would think to myself: *Well, I won't be doing that. I can barely stay in the chair long enough to write songs.* I have made a long and meaningful career as a singer/songwriter and recording artist. I have occasionally contributed essays to magazines and compilations, but the idea of writing an entire book was overwhelming, and any thoughts in that direction were shoved aside immediately—until Olga.

Olga Samples Davis, a writer and poet I met at Laity Lodge in the Texas Hill Country, decided for reasons known only to herself, that the time had come for me to write a book. To that end, every time we crossed paths, she would good-naturedly and somewhat relentlessly ask: "How's that book coming?"

I would respond, fairly tersely: "What book? There is no book."

She would smile and say: "Oh, there will be. I know it. It's time."

I was utterly puzzled by this—what did she care? But she did and she kept on.

A couple of years ago, again at Laity Lodge—a favorite place of refuge and sea changes for my family—she asked me again.

Later that same afternoon I went for a walk and, as I often do, began talking to myself: "Why are you so resistant to this? What are you afraid of?" Shortly into the walk, I received an invitation into my own story that dropped into my mind in the shape of the opening sentence to chapter one. I thought to myself: *Well, maybe I'll try a few pages.*

Gradually and reluctantly and with a great deal of hemming, hawing, and complaining, I surrendered to telling my tale. Every time I thought it was too much and that I would quit while I was behind, someone in the following group would come along to reignite the tiny spark and get me through a couple more chapters.

I received an offer to return to Laity and lead worship at a writer's conference in exchange for a memoir workshop with Lauren Winner. Lauren's books are on my shelves—well-read and much loved—so I jumped at the chance. It turns out that she is as gifted a teacher as she is a writer, and I gained a good deal of direction in a short period of time. But perhaps the greatest gift she gave me was encouraging me that I had an authentic voice as a writer and a story to tell. I started in with my usual monologue about how unbelievably hard it was to produce a book and who did I think I was anyway to imagine that I had something of value to say? She waited until I wound down and then gazed at me for a moment before saying: "Do it or don't." I cannot begin to say how helpful this was.

Lauren also supplied the opportunity for me to attend a longer writing class, this time at the Glen Workshop in Santa Fe, an annual arts conference sponsored by *Image* journal.

In doing this she gave me not only further instruction in writing but also opened up a whole new world of people and art that I knew little about and instantly connected with.

Kathleen Davis Niendorff knew about me through my album of hymns. She invited me to Austin to play a concert at her church. She did not know that I was working on a memoir; if she had known, she might not have invited me. She is a longtime literary agent and was not necessarily looking for a new client. As a matter of fact, when I offered her my first chapter along with the announcement that I was working on a memoir and could use an agent, she accepted it with silence—no encouragement, no discouragement, no nothing. I left an envelope with my first chapter on her kitchen table and drove out of Austin thinking that I was an idiot to be so bold and that I just needed to keep this book thing to myself.

To my utter surprise she called a few days later and left a message that went something like this: "Hello, Ashley, this is Kathleen. Well, when you told me you were working on a memoir, I thought to myself: *'Great. Just what the world needs— another memoir.'* But then I read it and I thought: *'Great! Just what the world needs—another memoir!'* Send me more chapters." Somewhere around chapter five, she signed me and began interfacing with publishers.

I met Don Pape when he was with Waterbrook. I had received an invitation from a writer named Constance Rhodes to contribute an essay to her book *The Art of Being*. Don liked my writing and made it a point to keep in touch with me. When Kathleen began shopping my manuscript in earnest, it was Don who came to the table with an offer that was generous and serious.

Those are a few of the significant people in the life of this effort. Here are the rest:

Thanks to my family and friends and particularly my mother, Burney, my sister Windsor, and my cousin Neel, who have all endured this invasion of privacy without a word of complaint—at least, not to me.

Thanks to my mother and my oldest friend, Leslie McMahon, who kept nearly every letter I had ever written them, dating back to the third grade. These were crucial for filling in some fairly wide blank spots.

Thanks to Constance, Becky Sowers, and Lydia Hutchinson for supplying some of my initial opportunities to write and be published.

Thanks to the first wave of readers: Cary Umhau, Kathleen, Deb Taylor, Steven and Amy Purcell, and my editor, John Blase. I could not have been in better hands.

Thanks to my endorsers—all trusted friends. I knew that if they couldn't say anything nice, they wouldn't say anything at all.

Thanks to DL Taylor for the cover. I have loved and owned her art for years. I knew that if she did the cover, people would be drawn to it. I was right.

Thanks to my beloved children who are all that I could have hoped for in this world.

And always, thanks to Kenny. He is the one whose opinion I value most. He knows me well, he sees me clearly, and he has devoted much of his time and attention to enhancing my gifts with his own in every area of our life together. He has not always been thanked for urging me to a deeper investment in writing and music—often my initial response is: "Who asked you?" But I am keenly aware that he has pushed me to places that have enriched me deeply, and he has taken much pleasure from the results. Me, too.

Finally, thanks to you, dear reader, for holding this book in your hands.

LITTLE BLACK SHEEP

The boy told the Shepherd: There's a fearful storm.
So I went out to the field to drive the flocks home.
I counted every lamb into the keep,
all except for one,
that little black sheep.

Chorus:
Little black sheep, little black sheep
in the howling wind with no relief.
In a cold, cold world, nothin' sounds so sweet
as the voice of the Shepherd to a little black sheep.

Little black sheep, she ain't nothin' but trouble.
She's not worth much, and she'll cost you double.
Shepherd says he knows, but he won't sleep.
He's gonna go out and find
that little black sheep.

Chorus

Now the little black sheep was the wandering kind,
but the Shepherd brought her back every time.
Mama says: Child, when your pride starts to creep,
you best remember, we all just
little black sheep.[1]

Chorus

RUBIN'S VASE AND THE GOD-SHAPED HOLE

I was recently providing music at a conference where one of the speakers, a noted professor of theology, remarked that we are in the "Experiential Age" of the Christian faith, an age that is defined by a professed personal relationship with Christ. Then she threw up her hands and said: "What does that mean?" Initially I thought she was distinctly in the wrong line of work, but then I found it to be a provocative question and thought: *Yes, what does it mean?*

I reflected on the idea of the God-shaped hole, the empty space in us that longs for the Lord and can only be satisfied with His Spirit. You could say that this concept is too small, that God wants to inhabit our whole being, not just our Sunday-morning best. But I think of it as negative space that, like Rubin's vase, reveals an entirely new subject. The God-shaped hole in me was the portal of my longing to be named, to be claimed, and to be loved. I could not find satisfaction for my desire anywhere else in this world. I did, however, give it my best shot. But my solutions led me to alcoholism, drug addiction, lying, cheating, stealing, promiscuity, and really bad moods. I spent years heaping shame upon shame.

Today my knowledge of Jesus is an abiding presence that is marked, often, by an overwhelming experience of the love and sense of place that I yearned for. Here I find acceptance and welcome, and over time, I have been changed. I see the evidence of transformation most vividly in my desire to love and serve others. I have been exclusively devoted to all manner of self-interest, self-will, and selfish living for the better part of my life, so the emergence of this outward gaze and concern—both at home and at large—is truly supernatural. Of course, I am not completely over myself, not by a long shot, so I expected to see the changes in my life spelled out in victorious living and attributes. Or as Jim Carrey's Grinch would say, I expected to be "joyful *and* triumphant." But that is not what happened.

The path I have taken is the low road of the gospel where I live as a broken person among the broken and where repeated failures have provided the Ebenezer stones for the things that I most cherish. I assumed that in coming to faith, my cracks and splits would be sewn together again in a seamless, saint-like fabric, but such is not the case. Much like the Velveteen Rabbit, I am a series of threadbare patches, irregular stitches with the stuffing poking out, and one button eye displaced and downcast.

I have serious issues with this.

I have despised my brokenness and cry out to God regularly and petulantly, particularly after a public display of contempt, shame, greed, gluttony, grandiosity, or insensitivity: "Would it be such a big deal to relieve me of some of this? Could You make me just a little less broken?"

The answer that I perceive is always the same: "No. More broken."

Over time I have come to understand that out of this ruined place comes every valuable thing that I have to give away. Here I see the foolishness of thinking that I should be in charge of anything, including, and perhaps most notably, myself. Here my notion of goodness is off the table, and I can only cling to Christ. And in the clinging I become teachable; I gain compassion and empathy; I am forgiven; I am free.

This is the story of the groundwork that paved the way to my faith. It is not an easy story to tell, but I have made my peace, and I do not "regret the past nor wish to shut the door on it."[2] Or, as the apostle Paul puts it: "By the grace of God I am what I am, and His grace toward me was not in vain" (1 Cor. 15:10). To that I would add: I am what I am and most of the time I would not be otherwise.

Every diver knows there's a lot at stake
But to the depth he goes as the water breaks
And for every shipwreck
There's a pearl he takes

Chained to the past
Chained to the fear

Chains on the floor
Broken for years
Freedom is calling me
And my heart races
I feel it in the broken places[3]

CHAPTER 1

· ·

SEVEN ARTS
AND SORROW

Tennessee

I wonder if my mother had any clue that she was marrying a man who had little or no interest in her substance, a man whose desire for her was fully satisfied in the superficial gloss of her Seven Arts skills. The Seven Arts, claiming that "To be poised, lovely, and well-groomed is the inherent right of every woman," was a local finishing school that offered a social navigation compass in manners and feminine wiles. My mother taught classes with such titles as "Gracious Physical Comportment," "Personality Development," "Basic Rules for a Pleasant Speaking Voice," "Hair," "Make-up," and "Wardrobe and Figure Control" to newly minted young society women at Rich's Department Store in Knoxville, Tennessee—the city where I was born.

My mother is not a classic beauty. She complains of small eyes, skimpy lashes, and too much fullness in her face. These days she says that when she smiles, her eyes disappear and she looks like a boiled egg. She has thick wavy hair, a full mouth, a fine figure, and great legs. But her secret weapon, developed over a long history in fashion and modeling, is an enviable understanding of how to put herself together so that her liabilities retreat into the shadow of her assets. My husband, Kenny, likes to say that when he met my mother for the first time, he realized he'd hit the jackpot by marrying into a family where the women continue to bloom well into their twilight. Now approaching eighty, she was and is quite a package.

I wonder if my father ever considered the utter futility of a dual, duplicitous lifestyle. He was a brilliant, complicated man, the product of a Southern matriarchal family with a domineering mother and a silent specter of a father. He escaped the small-town confines of Sweetwater, Tennessee, and earned a degree in Architecture at Yale and then a second degree in Interior Design at the University of Tennessee. He served as a second lieutenant in World War II, an event that he spoke little about except to say that he was in Patton's army. He was handsome, accomplished, charming—and gay. He met my mother in church, found her to be his equal in style and form, and married her, dreaming, I'm sure, of all the gracious living and fabulous parties that awaited them. He was not looking for intimacy with my mother; he was a man who viewed women as accessories or lapel pins: connected at the surface but meant only for display. When he fell for my mother, it was her presentation skills that won his heart. But he reserved the most honest, accessible part of himself for a secret male world fueled by good gin, where sex, glamour, gossip, and luxury fabrics were what mattered most.

Fortunately for my sister Windsor and me, my father's view of the perfect marriage included children, and we unwittingly came tumbling, two years apart, into a well-designed house-hold that had already begun to reek of alcohol and silence. My parents were highly visual and reverentially partial to physical and material beauty, which resulted in two pairs of fiercely critical eyes shining brightly in equal parts devotion and expectation on us. We were dressed to match, and I'm sure that plans for our debuts into society were hatching while we were still toddlers. We felt the weight of their attentions and also a darker calling, because though we knew nothing of the psychology of family systems, those dynamics were firmly in place, and we stepped neatly into our roles. Windsor was as good as gold in pursuit of their approval and became the family hero. I took the low road reserved for the scapegoat and provided plenty of ongoing distraction from the issues at hand by acting out our collective pain and dysfunction.

I have a friend who describes her family as "… all alcoholics except my brother, who's a Baptist." Mine was a similar drinking dynasty with legendary stories, such as the Halloween when one relative came to the door drunk and naked to greet the trick-or-treaters. She eventually left the candy bowl to her husband and retired to the bedroom where she would call for him repeatedly to come and attend to her. When he failed to answer, she set the house on fire.

My parents were both alcoholics; both were extraordinarily functional for the better part of their drinking careers. I understood the importance of the cocktail hour at an early age, and I have a snapshot memory of tasting my mother's Budweiser as she sat at her dressing table, preparing—in more ways than one—to go out for the evening.

I know that faith and the Presbyterian Church were a central part of our lives, but I have only the dimmest recollection of these things in my early childhood. In the South, nearly everyone attends church because it is an indication of good breeding and social standing. A genuine encounter and subsequent relationship with Jesus is not only unnecessary, but it is often considered overwrought and even a bit common. My mother had experienced that very genuine encounter as a child, though, and carried her faith into adulthood, passing it on to us in such a way that it never occurred to me to doubt the gospel, and I was particularly drawn to the Baby Jesus cradled in the crèche. But I viewed God the Father as a slightly larger and more impersonal version of my parents, carrying a measuring stick that quickly turned into a rod of reproof. The idea of an Abba who loved me and had plans of a future and a hope for me was utterly alien, and I assumed that if He knew my name at all, it was because He had heard that my behavior was so bad my mother had resorted to having me cut my own switches.

Inevitably, my parents' marriage collapsed. My mother made a valiant effort to keep it alive by insisting on marriage counseling, but she was urging my father to places he had no intention of going, and although he was physically present for the sessions, he refused to participate or even to speak. This pattern continued nearly to the end of his life; he had still waters running deep, but he wasn't able to access them and confined himself to the shallows that swirled around him like party chatter and never rose above his ankles.

They divorced when I was in kindergarten; their final argument was precipitated by some mischief I had gotten into early one morning. I had collected my mother's liquid makeup and lotions and mixed them all together into a pinky-beige mess. My father got up and came into the spare bathroom where I was occupied to take a shower but didn't notice the telltale bowl or empty containers, because I had hidden them behind a large box of laundry detergent. My mother discovered it all fairly quickly when she awoke and accused my father of avoidance—a path he regularly took throughout their marriage and a source of tension and resentment for my mother. They fought briefly and my father left, returning only once to pack his belongings.

My mother punished me severely that morning, spanking me and shoving me under my bed to retrieve the caps to the smeared, empty bottles that littered the bathroom. Windsor retreated to the farthest corner of the conflict. She was silent, watchful, and good as gold. After the furor, my mother came to me with a tearful apology, but though I have understood for many years that her grief and rage had little or nothing to do with my part in the whole event, I continue to carry the weight of responsibility for their divorce in the earliest, most fragile images of my childhood. The head is no match for the heart in these formative experiences, and if there was a jumping-off place for me into shame and self-destruction, this was it.

My mother went to work as a traveling saleswoman in the fashion industry and brought in a succession of caregivers, most of them African-American. Some of these women were loving and nurturing to me, and in many ways, they became my other mothers. I particularly loved a handsome woman named Eva who worked for my grandparents, and once in a while, she would take Windsor and me home with her to spend the weekend. We would help her husband, George, in his garden, play with the neighborhood children until after dark, and then collapse in a giant four-poster in Eva's front bedroom. It was a world away from the trouble and confusion in my own home, and I pestered her often to let us go with her when she left for the day.

My grandfather was a devoted fly fisherman and had, as a young man, won the money in a poker game to purchase a cabin in a little community called Elkmont, located in the Great Smoky Mountains about an hour from Knoxville. He and my step-grandmother spent the better part of their summers in Elkmont, and I found another refuge there on the Little River, which roared beside our cabin. My sister and I, and our friends, rode the water like rainbow trout, shivering with the cold and thrill. Near the banks, away from the current, we would stack stones to create tranquil, glittering pools where we bathed and washed our hair. Then we would lie on a flat, warm rock in the middle of the river, breathing in the sulfur-soaked air, feeling the flick of the spray and dreaming.

In Knoxville, we were surrounded by the love and support of extended family and friends, and my mother provided as much stability as she could for us. But the upheaval of our lives and the inattention that often accompanies a focus on survival was reflected in the fates of our pets, all of which came to a bad end.

Our first dog, Richard, ran away, and our next dog, Grover, was hit and killed by a car. He was lying in the road at the bottom of our driveway when I came home from school one day while my mother was out of town. Then there were the baby chicks that we got for Easter one year that were promptly eaten by the one-eyed, three-legged dog, Spunky, who lived next door. I hated that dog.

My father continued building his career as a designer and simultaneously became a partner in a local furniture store that he referred to as his shop. He was faithful and constant in his own way to Windsor and me. He spent his Wednesdays and every other weekend with us, showered us with gifts, and never missed a child-support payment. He had an iron will bent toward propriety, seeking and finding his safe footing in doing the right thing, which is similar to modern political correctness—a polite framework but, by itself, disingenuous and ultimately meaningless. So although he was impeccably mannered and tended to the smallest social obligation with the confidence of a man who intrinsically understands the written and unwritten rules, the emotional truth that creates intimacy was nowhere to be found, making him distant and ultimately unknowable.

But then I was just a little girl, and he was my daddy, handsome and on time. He smelled good and took me to the Golden Arches anytime I wanted. He let me get black-licorice ice cream at Dipper Dan's and played his show-tune records for me over and over again. And though my first few years of life were equal parts love and chaos, Knoxville was in many ways a safe haven for me. It was a small world where I could run away from home in my mother's high heels and clatter down the street to my friend Leslie's house, where I would be taken in and given lunch. It was a place where every landmark and every kid in my neighborhood was familiar to me, where there was an awareness of the ache within my family and an extended community that responded as they were able. Those days offered the closest thing to normal that I would experience for a very long time, but just as I was beginning to have a sense of place and belonging, the twig of stability I was clinging to snapped, and we moved.

CHAPTER TWO

A BLACK-AND-WHITE RAINCOAT IN A STRANGE LAND

California

My mother worked for a company called Shu-Mak-Up. They manufactured small jars of paint, glitter, and luster powder formulas that were meant to transform shoes, handbags, and even gloves into color-matching wardrobe accessories. The idea was that a woman could add ongoing fashion excitement to her ensemble by painting and repainting the same items according to the outfit or occasion. Their slogan was: "One, two, color your shoe with Shu-Mak-Up."

She covered the state of Tennessee, and her sales record with department stores and boutiques was so impressive that the company, in a grassroots expansion effort, offered to relocate her anywhere in the continental United States she cared to go. She chose San Francisco and left for six weeks to find a place for us to live. She returned home with stories of the ocean—which we had never seen—cable cars, and the Golden Gate Bridge, hoping to spark tiny flames of curiosity and anticipation in us. But her job began on the second of January, and she had calculated that in order to arrive in San Francisco on time but still spend as much of the holiday season as possible in Knoxville, we would need to leave on Christmas morning as soon as the last present had been opened. Upon hearing this news, whatever excitement I might have felt quickly turned to alarm. "Christmas?! Christmas Day??!! Mommy, no!"

Nevertheless, on December 25, 1964, in the middle of my third-grade year, my mother, my sister, our maid, Dorothy, and I all piled into our gray Chevy Nova. Dorothy heaved herself into the backseat, showing everything but her agility. She expressed her own extreme anxiety over leaving Tennessee in outbursts of flatulence resulting in daily skirmishes between Windsor and me over who would ride next to her.

Dorothy had good reason for concern. Soon after we crossed the state line into Little Rock, Arkansas, we stopped at a diner to eat and were refused service because we were in the company of a black woman. Dorothy retreated with me to the restroom, crying and shaking so badly she couldn't get a grip on the faucet to wash her hands. My mother, on the other hand, had a firm grasp on her Southern charm and powers of persuasion, and she eventually shamed the waitstaff into serving us. But Dorothy's trembling continued unchecked, and she left the restaurant wearing most of her meal on her uniform.

Despite the inhospitable start, we kept going day after day, crossing time zones, crossing cultures, driving over plains and deserts and through a sudden flash flood, until we finally reached the mysterious city with its Spanish name and bridge made of gold.

When we arrived in San Francisco, my initial disappointment in discovering that the Golden Gate Bridge was actually red was consumed in the excitement of being in a big city. While waiting to move into our new house, we had an extended stay at the Cable Car Motel on Lombard Street. Lombard itself is somewhat magical, having the distinction of being one of the world's curviest roads. We wandered around different areas of the city, like Fisherman's Wharf, expanding our Southern "meat and three" palates with cracked crab and sourdough bread, and landed at the Ghirardelli Chocolate Manufactory, where the ice-cream sundaes were the size of my head. I was mesmerized by the spectacle of it all and would have been content to continue there indefinitely, diverted and enticed by the endless pleasures of the moment with nothing before and nothing beyond, like a perpetual vacation bubble. But reality led out of the city and a few miles up Highway 101.

We settled in Marin County just north of San Francisco on an island called Belvedere, which lies between the Tiburon Peninsula and Richardson Bay. The house my mother leased was a landmark called the Pagoda House in a nod to its shape. It was old and creaky with an overhang that jutted out like the bridge to nowhere. It seemed as if it was clinging to the island solely by its notoriety, and when the wind blew or earthquake tremors shook the ground, I waited for the inevitable slide. The house had better foundations than I did, though, and held firmly to its place in the world.

In January, I started at the local elementary school as a person of interest with my East Tennessee accent and innocence. But I was a brokenhearted child, and a dislocated one at that, with no idea how to stake a claim in this strange, beautiful place. Children have keen eyes for weakness and my classmates quickly spotted my vulnerability and lack of confidence. When the initial attention faded to disinterest and ultimately disdain, I accepted the rejection and formed proximity friendships with neighbors and other kids who occupied the social margins.

My mother was a big-occasion gal and took full advantage of Bay Area culture, which was as brilliant as the sunlight on the water surrounding it. We took dance and art lessons at the San Francisco Museum of Modern Art. We rode the ferry across the bay into the city and picnicked in Golden Gate Park where we became members of the zoo and received our own elephant-shaped keys. My mother took a turn as a Girl Scout leader despite the indignity of the uniform, which she described as "swamp green," a color that, in her opinion, could not be salvaged. She excelled in field trips, such as an excursion to the Presidio in San Francisco to visit the parade grounds for a flag ceremony. She lectured us repeatedly about being on our best behavior for this solemn occasion, but when the cannons exploded, she was the one who jumped the highest and sprawled the widest.

On my own time I discovered the solace of solitude and took solo expeditions exploring Belvedere Island, where I would wander the narrow roads, inhaling the scent of eucalyptus. I spent time on Point Belvedere watching the seals play on the rocks below, and built forts in the untended areas around our house, where I learned the hard way what poison oak leaves look like but also began imagining a rich, episodic fantasy life where I was the much-beloved and sought-out center of attention.

My mother eventually changed jobs and went to work in the fashion industry, coordinating runway shows and editorial layouts for Union Square department stores like I. Magnin and Macy's. She worked as a stylist for the Grimme Agency on Grant Avenue, the city's oldest street, teaching diminished heel switches and body position to the young, lithe models. She herself modeled for organizations like the Junior League at charity events over the years, and her runway experience served her well. She excelled in "pushing with her show foot" in nearly every area of her life.

Windsor and I also modeled occasionally on the boards and in print, and I would point out the pictures in the Sunday magazine of the *San Francisco Chronicle* to my classmates, hoping to impress them and improve my desirability cachet. Fashion-forward photographs didn't carry much weight at Reed Elementary School though, and I was unwittingly fueling contempt rather than admiration.

The tipping point arrived wrapped in a black-and-white patent-leather raincoat, cap, and boot set that I received for my birthday. I wore it to school exactly once, walking in the door to a gaping classroom audience that was resourceful enough to have a well-placed thumbtack waiting for me in my desk chair by the time I left the coatroom. It was all I could do to keep from howling into the grinning silence that followed.

On another day, I arrived at my homeroom to find my desk was missing. I found it eventually, poking up out of the tall grass on the side of a hill next to the school like one of those puzzles where you find the thing that doesn't fit. I dragged it back to my classroom along with another layer of shame, thinking that tomorrow and the next day and possibly the one after that, I might need to stay home sick. I don't know that my vocabulary included the word *despair*, but my stomach was well acquainted with the feeling.

I continued a pattern of acting out at home, bullying my sister and the handful of neighborhood kids who were in a weaker position than I was. It seemed that every little thing conspired to keep me from belonging.

My mother was progressive in her eating habits and aware of my increasing lack of control in my own consumption, so she refused to buy Wonder Bread, the pillowy white bread that was the gold standard of sandwiches in those days. I had whole-wheat bread with tuna, which I hated, an apple, and skim milk, so I would just throw the whole thing in the trash can, prompting one of my teachers to retrieve my lunch sack from the garbage, call me up to the front of the class, and make an example of me as an ungrateful child who threw away a perfectly good lunch. He would then pull out and display each food item, which the class looked upon with disgust. Brown bread? Gross. Tuna fish thick with mayonnaise? Gross. Ashley? Gross.

One afternoon I refused to put my lunch box away when I got home from school, and Dorothy threw it at me in frustration. I phoned the local police and told them that our maid was trying to kill me. They dispatched an officer, who found me hiding in a closet with the dog and lectured me about appropriate and inappropriate use of law enforcement.

Poor Dorothy got the full force of my growing anger. She struggled with her own lack of stability and community; ultimately she experienced a psychotic breakdown, and my mother sent her back to Knoxville to live out her days in a state institution. After that, we had a succession of helpers, none of whom were as nurturing or close to me as the ones I had known in Knoxville.

My mother remarried when I was ten. My stepfather was a transplanted Midwesterner and accomplished attorney who had established himself in the Bay Area with a practice in San Rafael. He'd also had a stint as mayor of Mill Valley and several terms as a Golden Gate Bridge director. He had been orphaned early in life and shuttled around to family members in Indiana, eventually being raised by an aunt and uncle in an atmosphere that was long on duty and short on affection. As a result, he was a stern, unyielding man prone to depression. My mother's humor and vivacity were tonics to his gloom, and he adored her. He accepted us as part of her package and, in truth, made an effort to step into the role of parent. He and I were oil and water though, and I, for one, wasn't having it. I had been more or less running my own show with my frazzled working mother and absent father, and the entrance of a strict authoritarian triggered even more rebellion that expanded to include stealing from shops in downtown Tiburon. My fits of rage led to violence, and my mother and stepfather began to get calls regarding various incidents of hitting other children.

One of those incidents occurred at an ice-skating rink. I was there for a birthday party and got into an argument with an older girl out on the ice. I lost my temper and kicked her in the shin with my skate. The result was an injury that required stitches and a narrowly avoided lawsuit for my parents. I regularly lost all privileges and spent a good deal of time confined to my room. I didn't want to be a bad kid, but I didn't want to be a good kid either. I hated the way I felt inside, and I just wanted to feel different.

Shortly after my parents' marriage, we moved to a larger house on Belvedere where I was eventually able to occupy a mother-in-law suite on the bottom floor that conveniently included its own entrance and exit. Now I didn't mind being sent to my room. I knew I wouldn't be staying there long.

At the close of each school year, my mother would drive Windsor and me to the airport to board a red-eye to Atlanta where we would change planes with the help of an escort for Knoxville and stay until Labor Day. My father would drop us off at the local swim club nearly every morning just before it opened and pick us up in the evening after work. On the days we stayed at home, Sevaria and Brenda would babysit. They were the nieces of my beloved Eva, who still worked for my grandparents and continued to provide a place of refuge for me when I was in Knoxville. Sevaria and Brenda were teenagers and arrived at my father's house with a stack of 45 records, introducing us to the music of Marvin Gaye, Stevie Wonder, the Supremes, and James Brown. We made the needle skip on our portable record player, flinging ourselves around trying to follow their practiced dance steps, wearing out the little strip of red carpet in our loft bedroom.

Several weeks of each summer were spent in the Smoky Mountains with my maternal grandparents, Papa and Mama D.

Papa had built a regional chain of children's shoe stores called Paul Parrott Shoes out of his own third-grade education. Windsor and I took sewing lessons at one of his stores where we chatted with Cookie the mynah bird, whose vocabulary consisted of: "Hi, honey," "I think I'll take a bath," and "I think I'll have dessert." I thought I would have dessert too—often—as I discovered the emotional companionship of food, which acted as stimulant, sedative, entertainment, and antidote all in one sublime and usually vacuum-sealed package.

Papa married Mama D. after my grandmother died of cancer. She was a blue blood from Connecticut, descended from the first pilgrims and carrying titles like Colonial Dame and Daughter of the American Revolution. She used to say, regarding Elkmont, that she didn't much care for the fish, but she loved the fisherman, so she happily spent her days in her trademark bright colors with matching shoes, sewing needlepoint on the screened-in porch and reading trashy books about all kinds of forbidden love, accepting the minimal cabin comforts and occasional bear or snake intrusion for his sake.

My grandfather's passion was fly-fishing; he left the cabin every morning in his waders, chasing amateur fishermen with their jars of live bait off of the mountain and bringing home a creel of rainbow trout at the end of the day that he would clean, roll in cornmeal, and fry in a cast-iron skillet. Patience was not his virtue, so he spent little or no time teaching us to fish, but we were busy with our own exploits, learning the Little River boulder by boulder. We sped over the rapids in fat black inner tubes down to the swimming hole where we leapt off of the scraggy cliff ledges to impress the boys. I felt a lightness in my heart there, like a perfect skipping stone skimming the water with hardly a splash, and I would leave a piece of my soul wedged between the mossy rocks each time we headed back down the mountain.

My father's family was from Sweetwater, a small town between Knoxville and Chattanooga. My grandfather worked at the local furniture store while my grandmother ran the show from her kitchen, filling us with fried chicken and biscuits, boiled custard, and chocolate sheet cake when we came for a visit. We played Rook with my grandfather in the evening and sat with him on the porch while he smoked, mostly to escape the *Lawrence Welk Show*, which my grandmother adored, but personally, I discovered my tolerance for polka music was right around zero.

In Knoxville, I was something of an exotic, a California girl, albeit one with distinct traces of a Southern accent. Never mind that my West Coast status was strictly no account, never mind that Knoxville was my hometown. When I arrived from the land of surf and sun, suddenly I was new.

On his days off, my father would take us skiing on the lake. He would fill a cooler with Bermuda onion sandwiches and half-gallon containers of vodka and grapefruit juice. We would each invite a friend, and he would bring one or two of his own friends. He would dock his ski boat on a small island where we swam and played cards while my father and his companions drank and unselfconsciously sunbathed in bikinis that were skimpier than Speedos.

At the end of the day, we would return home, where my father would shower and dress to go out for the evening. His life was defined socially, and whenever there was a party or event given by a person of note, he would say that if you weren't on the guest list, you might as well pack your bags and leave town. He needn't have worried; he was the perfect guest, beautiful to behold and a master at repartee, not to mention able to hold his liquor. Thus he maintained a crowded dance card, sometimes escorting local divorcees or widows but more often going stag with his friend and business partner, Jim.

He kept mostly male company with only the occasional and much-discussed date with a woman. He spoke of a mysterious lady love in Atlanta named Roxanne and said he thought he might marry her one day, but I don't recall ever meeting her. And I don't remember when it dawned on me that he was homosexual. My awareness grew slowly, like grass, fed by random comments and whispers, fed by an endless succession of pretty men in short shorts and a distinct lack of female presence. I was naive about what being gay actually meant, but I knew he was different in a way that no one talked openly about, adding to my own feelings of dislocation.

Windsor and I continued as his lapel pins, occupying the rare open spots in his engagement book. We were unwittingly submerged in the secrecy of his life that ultimately was a secret only to himself. He maintained nearly to his death that he and my mother should never have ended their marriage and that it was all just a misunderstanding based on a lack of communication.

And even though Knoxville felt like home to me, anchored by family and my friend Leslie, who was my earliest and dearest childhood companion, I remained on the fringes as the summer visitor with the father who wasn't like other fathers, shuttled back and forth between grandparents, caregivers, and friends, belonging everywhere and nowhere.

Windsor and I would return to California at the end of each summer, loaded down with clothes from Rich's Department Store and, in my case, ten or fifteen extra pounds. My father replaced emotional availability with lavish gift giving, outfitting us with clothing and jewelry to excess. Then he would pack us up and put us on a plane, wiping tears from his eyes as he retreated behind sunglasses. I was equally moved and puzzled by his tears, but I think I understood then, as I do now, that to the extent that he was able, he loved us dearly.

In sixth grade I was flattered and surprised by the sudden attention of one of the popular boys in my class. The sweetness of this turn of events lasted around forty-eight hours before provoking vengeful hostility in an equally popular girl who happened to be wearing his ID bracelets. She used her considerable influence to stir up a playground mob, and I found myself one day at recess suddenly in the center of a large gang of kids on the handball court. They closed the circle and began throwing things at me, including rocks. Mercifully the bell eventually rang, and I hid in the girl's bathroom where an odd and universally disliked boy named Brandon, who had a nervous habit of pulling out his eyelashes, followed me to express his empathy and solidarity. His compassionate gesture only further reminded me of my bottom-rung position on the California public school food chain. I was not particularly hurt physically, but the event was a game changer emotionally, and I went out of my way to avoid groups of any kind afterward. And I took up smoking.

CHAPTER THREE
. . . .

GOOD AND EVIL, SIDE BY SIDE

California

In junior high school I settled into a more normal experience of adolescence, if one can call trying to navigate the emotional black hole and unwanted intrigue of puberty "normal." I wasn't particularly popular, but I wasn't much of a target either, and I had begun to develop a few interests that quickly became passions.

I discovered a love for horses at Penrose Farm in Knoxville, where my father would deliver me a couple of days a week to visit a family friend, Teenie. She eventually turned over the care and maintenance of one of her mares, Brown Betty, to me for the summer.

Back in California I mounted a relentless and ultimately successful campaign for a horse of my own, resulting in the purchase of an unbroken sorrel filly that I named Nickeloe. The time spent training and riding her was a welcome distraction from my loneliness and struggle to belong, and I had aspirations of a place on the show circuit, although neither of us was remotely show worthy. She was skittish and unpredictable, and I was graceless and too unsure of myself to give either one of us the confidence that might lead to competitive riding. I was far more suited as a stable girl, and I found great solace in grooming her and riding the trails that wound across the Tiburon hills, one misfit atop another.

My mother insisted on weekly church attendance, and my fiercest rebellion brought little more than an eye roll. I looked for any opportunity to annoy her during the worship service, loudly flipping through the hymnal, fidgeting like a toddler, and drawing on the registration pad. She paid little or no attention; her victory was getting us into the pew. After that, we were the Lord's problem.

We attended a little Presbyterian church in Tiburon where our pastor favored peace marches and a beatnik look, styling his iron-gray hair into a Prince Valiant cut and wearing turtlenecks and medallions. He was progressive (or foolish) enough to occasionally turn the service over to the youth group to lead music, and my participation did a lot to ease my hostility toward church attendance. We led the congregation with camp songs like "Rise and Shine" and Top Forty hits that vaguely suggested spiritual content to us like Three Dog Night's "Joy To The World."

Music was already essential to me. I had listened to my mother's records, like Nino and April's "Begin the Beguine" and *Meet the Beatles!*, with my ear pressed up against the hi-fi speaker since kindergarten and now spent nearly every dime of my allowance and babysitting money on vinyl 45s and LPs. I had some idea that I could sing and anticipated the youth services with an eagerness that was so fervent I would inevitably lose my voice on the big day and frantically spend the half hour before the service in the church kitchen bent over the sink gargling warm salt water. But even my hoarse attempts brought me something I hadn't experienced before: applause. And despite the fact that our set list was made up of material that only a parent could love, there was a genuineness in the response to my singing that sparked like flint. Here was a place to occupy apart from the larger group that I feared; here was a place I could have some semblance of control; here was something I had a natural talent for that brought a positive response and, I imagined, love and good wishes. I had unconsciously found my safety zone, and I grabbed every opportunity to turn the church dais into a stage.

I wasn't the only one taking advantage of opportunity. Sunday after Sunday, I believe the Lord was planting little seeds of faith in me—through the poetry and theology of the hymns, through the Sunday school Bible stories, through the kindness and inclusiveness of many of the church members. Thoughts of a personal God were still more sinister than inviting to me though. I had an uneasy suspicion that He was keeping track of every cigarette I lifted out of open packages, every pair of earrings I stole, every act of vandalism in late-night adventures sneaking out with my neighborhood friends, and planning an appropriate and devastating punishment. It would be many years before I understood that He called me by name and sought me as His own, but that foundation was laid.

A foundation for addiction was being laid as well, but I was equally unaware of it. My mother was a secret drinker, and though the big hand on her cocktail hour was gradually moving backward, her drinking had not yet taken over her days. My stepfather was not an alcoholic and, at that time, was unconcerned about my mother's drinking. The obvious dissolution of a family mired in addiction wasn't apparent in mine; it was more of a quiet, fuzzy detachment. My father had a legendary ability to hold his liquor and had built his design firm and personal career into a show-piece that shone in nearly every notable house in Knoxville. He drank regularly and heavily, but his constitution and force of will belied the seriousness of his situation. For both of my parents, the essential thing in life was maintaining the appearance of grace and refinement. And the drink, well, that was just the shiny cherry that aided and added merriment and ease. They seemed far more concerned with my appearance than any of their own issues.

My eating binges, which had begun in grammar school, had accelerated in adolescence, and my letters to Leslie back in Knoxville cataloged one diet after another. Atkins, grapefruit and hard-boiled eggs, Weight Watchers, diet pills—the list was endless and fruitless. No model in a magazine, no offer of a new ward-robe, no chubby snapshot could compare to the comfort, pleasure, and power to wipe the emotional slate briefly clean that I found in food. My father would call us periodically during the school year and often his greeting to me would be: "How's your weight?" rather than: "How are you?" Not surprisingly, it was going up. The truth was that I had already lost the power of choice in the matter and nothing he or my mother said was going to change that anytime soon.

I walked into Redwood High School as a freshman, fourteen years old and weighing 163 pounds. I cast about the large student body looking for a place to belong and eventually settled in as a handmaid to one of the loveliest, most popular girls. She, too, had cultivated a lifestyle of sneaking out at night, smoking, and stealing, so we fit together neatly in that regard. She had also begun to be sexually active, but aside from being briefly pawed by a pimply redneck whom I met at a hotel in South Carolina one summer, I'd had little or no experience with boys and was terrified of the prospect.

But I was all-in with illicit activity, and we expanded our thieving territory from the boutiques of downtown Tiburon to the department stores of San Francisco. I had already been caught and arrested a couple of times and sensed that I was more bumbling than badass in my fledgling life of crime, but the desire to be part of a cutting-edge group of girls was overwhelming, and I would not—could not—say no.

At school there was a small group of African-American kids who were bussed in from Marin City. They were understandably wary, usually on the offensive, and not to be messed with. I accidentally bumped against one of the largest, toughest girls with my tray in the lunch line one day, and and she accused me of staining her white jeans with a pomegranate. I couldn't see a single spot and foolishly got into an argument with her. She beat me soundly, surrounded by her posse, and told me I had better bring twenty dollars the very next day to replace the pants or she would beat me again till something broke. After that, she stalked me in the halls and would suddenly materialize in the girl's bathroom whenever I was there, slamming me up against the tile wall and demanding payment. I finally told my mother, who called the school. She was suspended indefinitely, and I didn't have much trouble after that, but my parents decided private school might provide a better environment. So I was enrolled in a Catholic girls' school as a day student my sophomore year. Initially my quarrel was only with the nuns, who were not amused by harmless pranks, such as convincing the school-bus driver to take us to A&W for a snack on his afternoon run. But eventually I managed to alienate nearly the entire school by stealing money out of a locker belonging to a popular senior.

When I was a small child, my great-grandmother told my mother that I had a tremendous capacity for good and for evil and only time would tell the tale. At San Domenico School for Girls, the Reverend Mother pronounced to my mother that time had told and the dark side had won. She encouraged my parents that the school was not a good fit for me, so I stayed for only a year, which was fine with me since I was a persona non grata among my peers, and no one had much to do with me after the locker incident.

My stealing career ended abruptly during Christmas break of my sophomore year. A group of girls went on a spree in San Francisco that ended in the office of a department-store detective, who kindly opted to call our parents rather than the police. The other parents were either not at home, not interested in hearing about it, or certain that the whole incident was somehow the store's fault. My mother, on the other hand, decided that the time for drastic measures had arrived. She insisted that I stand up in church the following Sunday during the time of sharing and prayer requests to report what I had done to the congregation. The room was packed with a number of college kids home for the holidays, and I could hardly breathe, let alone tell the story, because once again I was at the center of a group and expecting nothing but harm. I finished my tale, sobbing and gasping and wild to get out of the room. My parents also decided that I would receive no Christmas presents that year, so when my father's usual truckload of boxes arrived, they were promptly returned.

I never stole so much as a pack of gum after that, so I will say that the punishment was absolutely effective. I will also say that although I know my mother's intentions were good, public humiliation for a child, particularly a child already drowning in shame, may accomplish its short-term goal, but in the long run, it adds years to the problem. Losing the presents would have been enough.

One of the musicians at church taught me a handful of guitar chords, and I retreated fully into the world of music, buying songbooks and trying to pick out the tunes of albums I loved. Around the same time, I met an older girl named Laurel at Young Life who was one of the music leaders. Young Life is a nondenominational parachurch ministry that has an outreach to high school students, meeting weekly in homes for music, skits, and a low-key presentation of the gospel. Laurel had recently moved into an apartment close to my school, and I would often go by there in the afternoons, climbing through her window and waiting for her to get home from work so we could play guitar, smoke Sherman cigarettes, and marvel over Joni Mitchell's songs. The ease, admiration, and affinity that came my way through music were magic to me, and it quickly became my lifeline.

The summer following my sophomore year, having mastered five chords and five Neil Young songs, I talked my way into my first gig, playing for tips during lunch at a friend's brother's restaurant in Knoxville. I played the same five songs, over and over again, usually until someone offered me a dollar to take a break. I didn't mind though, I was fifteen and playing music for money. And just like that, the idea of a future was born, and from those days forward, my all-consuming fantasy involved a stage and a microphone. Not only had music supplied my identity and a safe distance from the crowd, the social skills I lacked and the loud boisterous way I operated to hide my unbearable awkwardness became unimportant. I could do something that other people couldn't do, and honey, I was going to do it day and night with all my heart.

In my junior year of high school, I returned to Redwood and carried on without any particular incident. My sister Jennie had arrived as a welcome surprise to my parents when I was thirteen, and she brought an air of sweetness to our home that was ripe with possibility. My parents decided that the time for a change had come and sold our house on Belvedere to relocate forty miles up Highway 101 to a ranch town called Petaluma. They bought a lovely old colonial on the west side, and I was enrolled in Petaluma High School in January. I stayed firmly on the social fringes and can only remember three or four kids from that period, all of whom were neighbors. I have even less memory of my classes or activities at school, but I do recall my English teacher, a dignified lady named Mrs. Stovall. She saw promise in me as a writer and took an enthusiastic interest, expanding my world with literature and encouragement.

I continued to learn guitar and played flute in the school band. I brought my horse to a pasture in Petaluma, but music had eclipsed my love of riding, and eventually I sold her.

I was exposed to drugs to some extent. Marijuana was the California teen drug of choice, and I certainly tried it a few times, but I didn't like the paranoia I felt with it. I was already uncomfortable in my own skin and using food to balance the scale. I didn't need any assistance there. Drinking was still off in the distance for me—I had begun to develop the extreme behaviors of alcoholism but hadn't yet struck the match.

I stayed in touch with my friends in Marin County, and once I had my driver's license, would head south periodically to meet up with them and go to concerts. One weekend, while my parents were out of town, we had plans to see Tower of Power at Winterland in San Francisco. After the show, I spontaneously invited several kids back up to my house, and the initial small crowd had doubled and then tripled by the time we reached the exit for Petaluma. Chaos ensued, fueled by drugs, drink, and nearly a complete lack of adult presence.

Our maid, Tempe, was staying with us, but she had no interest in crowd control and hid in my parents' bedroom with Jennie, shouting down the stairs periodically for us to stay out of the chicken she had fried earlier that day.

Windsor had a photographic memory for my bad behavior, one of the ongoing sources of contention between us. She anxiously watched the proceedings from a safe distance, assuring me she would tell Mom and Joe everything, *every*thing, if I didn't get these people out of the house. But her protests were fully ignored, and she finally took refuge in her own bedroom, blocking the door, I'm sure, with a chair. When everyone finally left near dawn, I got busy trying to mitigate the damages—scrubbing, polishing, and repairing as well as I could. I thought I had put everything to rights by the time my parents returned, but my mother's eagle eye immediately took stock of her belongings, landing on an antique armoire that now had a small piece missing. Her intuitive queries sounded like a battle cry to me, and before my sister or Tempe ever said a word, my mother had correctly summed up the situation, and she and I were arguing, then shouting, then slapping. No one was injured, but my stepfather decided that it was time for my father to share in the burden of parenting me and picked up the phone. He announced shortly after that incident that when I left for Tennessee the following summer, I would stay there to finish high school.

My father was initially annoyed and assured me there would be none of those shenanigans at his house. He could not have been more wrong. He hadn't the slightest idea about parenting an adolescent, unruly or otherwise, and paid only cursory attention to my curfew, school attendance, companions, and smoking habits. When I arrived in Knoxville, he announced that I would need a car to get to school and bought me a little Triumph Spitfire that had been repossessed by a local bank. I could not believe my luck.

When my mother regretted the hastiness of my dispatch to Knoxville later that summer and asked me to come home for another try, I quickly declined, claiming that a break would do us all good. I was enrolled in my fourth high school and settled into life in East Tennessee with the Bearden Bulldogs.

CHAPTER FOUR

. . . .

"NO PROBLEM"
IN A BOTTLE

Tennessee

California

The drinking age in Knoxville in 1973 was eighteen and remained as such for the next few years until the number of fatalities for teen drivers under the influence brought a hue and cry that could not be ignored. Meanwhile the adolescent good times in the Southeast rolled on.

I don't remember my first drink but I remember the feeling. It was a fountain of well-being containing all the things that I lacked: confidence, wit, fluidity, and ease in my conversation and movements. Suddenly the world sparkled, and I sparkled right along with it, like the perfect shimmer of foam bubbling out of a bottle of beer. All the events of my life to that point, swirling in the gene pool I had been born into, and with a strong-willed, all-or-nothing temperament priming the pump, thrust me toward that inevitable encounter. And once it was made, I was home. I had a true companion at my beck and call, massaging me, inspiring me, chasing away the dark melancholy tides crashing through my psyche, and setting me free to be ... Well, I had no idea. But after the third or fourth drink, it didn't really matter. I was hilarious, carefree, and fun, never far from the lamp shade.

The kids whom I had formed loose summer friendships with had abandoned the tennis courts and swim teams to cruise in overloaded cars down Cherokee Boulevard, a long road that ran the length of my neighborhood and skirted the Cumberland River. On the riverside, there were plenty of open grassy spaces with gravel parking areas, originally intended for more whole-some activities than piling up beer cans and cigarette butts, but teenage anarchy ran off anyone looking for a picnic spot, so the parking areas were nearly always empty and available.

My father's house was conveniently located right off the Boulevard. He made little or no adjustment to his lifestyle for the rigors of parenting, keeping nearly every square inch of his kitchen calendar filled with his elegant handwriting. I took advantage of his absence, offering my companions a place to retreat to when the beer ran out or the police arrived.

The house was a showplace, painted wall to wall in bright (or as my sister called it, "pee-pee") yellow, mixed with touches of Chinese red and yards of Italian Fortuny fabric draped across the windows and covering the accent chairs. The sofas were goose feather, upholstered in velvet, and even the smallest lamp or accessory was worth a small fortune. There was a fully stocked, never-locked liquor cabinet, which I offered freely to whoever came in the door. And come they did, happy to have such a nice place to practice opening their beer bottles with their teeth.

I had fallen into a group of Aigner-clad petite pretty girls and Izod khaki-wearing boys. In California, the teen culture reflected the free-love hippy era that had begun in the late sixties, featuring long, dirtyish, center-parted hair, tie-dye, embroidered Mexican shirts, sandals, and no bras. I was filling a D cup, and when I left my bra at home, I looked a lot more like my paternal grand-mother—breasts bouncing around my waist—than a fairy-like free spirit. I did my best to keep some semblance of the look going in Knoxville though, knowing that the Southern female's summer uniform of sundresses with spaghetti straps and Pappa Gallo flats, which made my feet look like overstuffed sausages, would only provoke me. I stuck to bandanas tied around my head and blousy Madras shirts with faded jeans, hoping that if I couldn't fit in, I could be different and cool.

I understood that I wasn't dating material for anyone in the crowd that I ran with, although I entertained constant fantasy crushes. But I was ready to ride shotgun on any given night, ready to agree to whatever foolishness was afoot, ready to be the last one to go home.

If my father had a curfew, he never mentioned it. He met me once coming in late, waiting in the foyer where I stumbled and fell at his feet. He turned without a word and disappeared in his bed-room, never mentioning the incident and never waiting up for me again. But he managed to read me the riot act through a lengthy measured silence that went on for nearly a week. His silences, as dismal and condemning as they were, had little or no impact on my actions though. Inside, I was longing to be claimed and filled like the empty parking spots on Cherokee Boulevard; outside, I was lit up like neon and blinking, Open All Night.

In the midst of that emotional mud puddle and my budding alcoholism, music remained. I expanded my repertoire beyond my initial five-song, five-chord set list and spent hours mimicking the artists I was listening to and then inhabiting their material with my own voice. I found new venues to play in, sporadically working for a few dollars in clubs up and down the Cumberland Avenue strip that ran through the University of Tennessee campus. I was thrilled with the opportunities to perform and even more thrilled with the access to unlimited cocktails. I was a well-developed sixteen and, with my low-tech, fake, paper ID, had no problem posing as an eighteen-year-old, no problem getting served, no problem getting drunk. No problem.

Needless to say, a well-traveled path between the bar and the stage does not bode well for any show, but my audience was running up its own tab and increasingly forgiving as the night wore on. I was full of teenage hubris, as well as confidence as a musician and, now, performer, but I was also aware that this ability that initially felt like magic to me was a gift. I had done nothing to earn it, and although I clung to it and relied on it as my sole source of value, I wasn't a particularly good steward of it. I played all the time but rarely practiced and tossed it aside easily when confronted with the choice between playing well and drinking more. And yet, I was getting better and better. Clumsy? Yes. Inconsistent? Absolutely. But this ability had taken on an expansive life of its own in spite of me, and because I believed in a Creator, I could only assume that He was also the giver.

I wasn't exactly sure how to square such generosity with the notion of a demanding, exacting God that I had carried with me like an ongoing threat. I was certain that the road I was on went straight to hell, and I fully expected to receive condemnation rather than cookies along the way. But my confusion over whom I might be dealing with did little at that point to draw me closer. My prayer life was confined to moments of despair when I was hungover or immobilized with shame about something I had said or done and ready to promise anything to get out of the hole. Once I was upright, I was off and running again—literally, figuratively, and spiritually.

My father was a member of Sequoyah Hills Presbyterian Church, which he attended every Sunday without fail and expected me to do the same. I don't know that his motivation was a desire for or an expression of a genuine encounter with the Lord; I don't know that he thought in those terms. But any conflict his not-so-secret activities suggested the moment he exited the sanctuary seemed to be no conflict at all. His only lapse in attendance over the years was due to his resentment at not being chosen to design a large addition to the sanctuary. That was a deal breaker. He spoke of how it really frosted him that the church Session would go with another architect after all his years of faithfulness, not to mention tithing. It took numerous visits from the senior pastor to restore him to his pew.

When I would ask my father about his faith, if he believed the gospel, if he knew Jesus, or what exactly he believed, he was simply silent. My mother, on the other hand, was fluent in her knowledge and understanding of the Scripture and spoke often of her faith, offering me Bible verses for comfort, encouragement, and without a doubt, instruction. I listened and parroted much of it as my own, because often it was lovely and hopeful. But ultimately it was her story, her good news.

She called frequently, and I was glad to hear from her because I missed her. I missed her cooking; I missed her affection and even her relentlessly sunny outlook, which had so often antagonized me; I missed her homemade pizza and the family gathering around the Sunday-night lineup on PBS. But not enough to put myself back under my stepfather's iron rule or to give up my new freedom, even though it often didn't feel much like freedom at all. I was driven, though not to life or anything life-giving, but to a depth of self-destructiveness that was irresistible and dreadful, and the powerlessness that had begun with food, now doused with alcohol, grew like kudzu.

My father's insistence on church attendance, much like my mother's in California, worked in my favor though. I found a ready audience there when I offered to play for the Wednesday-night services. I mixed contemporary songs from the Young Life songbook with hymns and spirituals and unwittingly supplied building blocks for some of the recordings that lay in my future. Equally foundational were the men and women who took an interest in me and encouraged my involvement in the church. They were glad to see me and went out of their way to invite me to Bible studies and socials. These small kindnesses so often seem insignificant to the ones extending them, but I have come to recognize how they reflect the beauty of the body of Christ, how each member fits together to make the whole, and how much can be accomplished in the life of another by a smile or an invitation. I received both and managed to participate somewhat regularly in the life of that church during my time in Knoxville.

I enrolled in Bearden High School and started as a senior in the fall of 1973. I joined a work-study program, along with the rest of my friends, called DECA, an acronym for Delta Epsilon Chi or Distributive Education Clubs of America. The purpose of the organization was identifying and training future entrepreneurs and leaders in the areas of finance, marketing, hospitality, and management. To that end, we would attend classes in the morning and work at jobs in our chosen fields in the afternoons. We might as well have called it Departing Education Campuses for Adolescents. Most of the kids in the class were fulfilling the job requirement by working for their fathers and viewed DECA as a convenient way to cut their classroom time in half.

I had no interest in or the slightest qualifications for any of the targeted areas of leadership development and declared a career path in rock and roll. I was told I would need to have some kind of supplementary afternoon job to participate in the program, so I would take waitress positions in an ongoing cycle of hiring and firing, prompted by my disdain for providing service in the service industry and for dealing with people in general. Mostly I would leave school with my friend Wilson and drive around listening to 8-track tapes of Jethro Tull, smoking, drinking, and definitely not working. I missed forty-five days of school that year.

And if my memory of classes at Petaluma High School is sketchy, I am at a complete loss to recall any classes at Bearden outside of the DECA classroom. I remember very little of my senior year in general, including my graduation ceremony, which came as something of a surprise to me considering my absences. I do remember not being asked to the senior prom and my utter relief at being invited to play a festival that weekend in another town. I remember my graduation party, where several families got together and rented the riverboat that ferried up and down the Tennessee River. There were tables of mostly untouched food, several kegs of beer, and a pure grain alcohol punch that came from a recipe provided by an enthusiastic parent. My father was one of the few passengers who managed to stay on his feet for the whole ride. The rest of us slid drunkenly from deck to deck on a punch-soaked floor, throwing up over the sides of the boat. This was one of the supervised parties.

Another clear memory is of a rare date with an older boy whose name and face are lost to me. Early in the evening he exclaimed, "Whoa, I just noticed your hands. They're huge! I bet they're bigger than mine; here, hold them up, let's compare." The shame that I felt over my size and shape was near constant. The urging from my parents and other family members to lose weight was near constant too. I spent time with my grandparents, and Mama D. would sit in her wingback chair ready to revel in whatever news I brought her. I would fill her in on upcoming events, and she would generally respond that I would need to start losing weight right away, because whatever the occasion, I would not want to attend it fat. She was right about that. I didn't want to go anywhere fat, but I relied on food to flatline the pain I felt over the way I looked. It is the vicious cycle of the addict: the source of our troubles is also the salve. Mama D. was plenty plump herself, which probably added to her fixation on my predicament, but she was also a wise lady and once said to me that she believed that I kept the weight on to protect myself from relationships I wasn't ready for, and when I was ready, I would lose it. She was also right about that. I was terrified to be loved and terrified I might never be loved.

My cousin Neel tells a story about a visit with my father once where she lamented her own weight problem and wondered if anyone would ever desire her enough to marry her. My father responded: "Oh, for heaven's sake, Neel. Unattractive people get married every day, just look at the Sunday paper!" Then he added that she better get busy with a diet, or he'd have to get her future wedding trousseau from Omar the tentmaker.

My father's view of humanity was comfortably black-and-white, dividing people into two groups: attractive and unattractive. And though the unattractive people had a place in this world and possibly even love and success, their stars were only bit players in the constellation and hardly glimmered at all. He, personally, was effortlessly thin and handsome throughout his life, and when he would press me with the mind-over-matter lecture, I would think: *Boy, that's rich. You just ate an entire bag of miniature candy bars for dinner.* But because he considered excess pounds inexcusable, the topic remained foremost in his mind, and once I was living under the same roof with him, his preoccupation with my weight, my clothing choices, my hairstyle—or lack of one—lit up like high beams.

Adding to my conflict was the unspoken sexual atmosphere in the household. My father was something of an exhibitionist and would often "relax" around the house or do his morning chores in bikini underwear. I knew on some level that his behavior, in light of the fact that I was living there, was peculiar and flagrant, but my presence had not inspired him to make any other changes in his manner of living, so I wasn't particularly surprised over his lack of a dress code. I did not consciously consider how living in a house that held a constant erotic charge might impact me. I was only concerned that he would be fully clothed if one of my friends showed up. I do know that I had no sense that my femininity was anything worth protecting or even respecting. Actually, I didn't have much sense of my femininity at all. I felt hardened to anything soft or womanly that stirred inside me; I didn't know what to do with it, and no one had ever led me to believe that it was valuable.

In spite of the beauty of my surroundings in my father's house, there was an atmosphere of oppressiveness that hung in the air like humidity, and though I couldn't define it, I could feel it. Once in awhile I would come face-to-face with it during some random activity, such as searching for matches in a drawer. In the midst of my rummaging, I would happen across photos, like pop-ups from a porn website, featuring my dad.

Looking back, it's easy, or easier, to remember the things that were painful, but there were also aspects of being there that were meaningful to me and had a stake in the course of my life. Being surrounded by extended family, my grandparents, and my cousins and having so many ties in the community restored some of the sense of belonging I had lost when we moved to California. For me, Tennessee would always be home. My father's housekeeper, Betty Rose, was a great friend to me and reminded me of some of the women who had filled my early childhood. We used to watch soap operas or "stories" together, keeping track of the latest bout of amnesia on *One Life to Live*. She was one of the rare people in my life who had no complaints about me except when I messed up a room she had just cleaned. She wrote me notes on occasion and let me stay home from school with her—although she said she had no business at all helping me play hooky. She was the choir director at her church, and sometimes she would teach me gospel songs, and we would sing together sitting at the kitchen table. I think she understood that I needed to have my spirit fed at that point in my life, perhaps more than I needed to mark time in a classroom.

And though it is easy for me to catalog the damage that my father inflicted, he continued to give as much as he had to give, faithfully providing all my material wants and needs and showing up to the smallest event. He would bring his friends to my club gigs, everyone tanned and smartly dressed. They clapped loudly, tipped lavishly, and ignored the beer-soaked floors and clientele. I think if anyone had suggested that he was anything less than a devoted, supportive father, he would have been genuinely shocked. I would have been shocked too. In truth, he was absolutely devoted to my sister and to me. However misplaced and corrupt his attentions were, he was still my daddy, and I didn't know any different. I didn't know that I was accepting cash in lieu of relationship, but I certainly had no problem doing it, and I was willing to live inside the puzzle of his world in exchange for having my own way on a daily basis.

But despite the thrill of doing as I pleased and the rootedness through extended family that I felt in Knoxville, the scales began tipping back toward the West Coast following high school. While music was my sole ambition, my peers were going to college, and my parents certainly expected me to do the same. I was a year ahead of my classmates, graduating when I was seventeen, so I decided to take some time off and return to California to try to figure out my next step. I had inflated ideas about going to Boulder, Colorado, or Cal Berkeley, but I didn't have the grades or the courage to realize any of those plans. I moved back into my parents' house in Petaluma just in time for the arrival of my brother, Paul, who was born that summer to everyone's delight.

I got a job at a small local music store, working for a creepy guy named Bill who consistently provided me with unwanted experience in sexual harassment. I was naive about the world and believed that bosses had the license to behave any way they wanted, so I gamely tried to either ignore or laugh at his dirty jokes and innuendoes. And working in a music store, no matter how two-bit, meant that I was in the music business and starting a career. I found opportunities to perform around Sonoma County, mostly providing background music during dinner, but I met other musicians and traded valuable musical information about songs and guitar techniques, which provided me with a world to disappear into during my free time.

The drinking age in California was twenty-one, and high-balls were not as easy to come by as they had been in Knoxville. As a secret drinker, my mother kept tabs on her wine jug levels to cover her own tracks, so the most I could hope to get away with at home was a can or two of beer. I found ways around it though, making friends with bartenders in the places I played, consorting with older musicians who could buy beer and wine for me, and even bussing tables at restaurants during my breaks, pretending to be helpful while finishing off half-empty glasses.

And the day came when I was happily introduced to cocaine, courtesy of Pierre, the owner of a small French bistro where I held a steady gig. Here was a stimulant containing an endless supply of false promises and the ideal companion to alcohol. Now I could drink longer; I could be a social genius, feigning intimate conversations with strangers; and I could feel powerful and in control all night long. Perfect.

CHAPTER FIVE
· ·

LOWER EDUCATION

Tennessee

My return to California was short-lived. After less than a year of residing under my parents' increasingly restrictive roof, of doling out strings and picks at the music store, of playing in noisy restaurants hoping to be heard in the rare conversational lulls, I was ready to re-relocate. The *geographical cure* is a well-known phrase in twelve-step circles, the idea being that our problems are centered on our immediate circumstances and that a change of address will wipe the slate clean and solve everything. Unfortunately there is another equally well-known phrase, "wherever we go, there we are," which is meant to serve as a reminder that the problem lies squarely within us. None of that registered with me though. All I knew was that I was unhappy where I was, tired of my mother's lectures and the accountability that she and my stepfather required. Suddenly college seemed like a very good idea and Knoxville shone in my memory like Elysium.

My father offered the path of least resistance, suggesting that I return and enroll at the University of Tennessee. Thus began another decade of ping-ponging back and forth between the East and West coasts. I packed up my current car, a Volkswagen Bug, and drove Interstate 40 all the way home.

The only high school courses I had even remotely enjoyed were creative writing and French, so I thought I would put together some kind of liberal arts major, but my primary concern was playing music. In California I had been denied access to work in clubs because I was underage, but in Knoxville I was eighteen and fully entitled. My father began including me in his evening cocktail hour, which was the only semblance of emotional intimacy that I enjoyed with him. His smile became a little brighter, his outlook a little cheerier, his talk a little looser and wickedly funny, though always at someone else's expense. He was not one to stagger or slur, at least not at that point, and maintained his well-heeled demeanor no matter what the reading on his blood alcohol level. There were telltale signs that the drink was in charge though, such as the morning I walked into the kitchen to find a highly pedigreed Saint Bernard puppy, which he had drunkenly paid a fortune for at a fund-raising dinner the previous night. He named the dog Alexander and lost interest in him almost immediately, eventually turning him loose to roam the neighborhood, 150 pounds of unlimited destruction in search of a snowcapped mountain. Alexander was a wily dog and survived his neglect for a couple of years before succumbing to the relentless heat and humidity of a Tennessee summer. A neighbor found him one morning in her front yard, another casualty in my family's dismal track record with pets.

In the fall of 1975, I moved into Carrick Hall and began college. Initially I made an effort to keep up with my classes, even making the Dean's List once or twice, but ultimately academics gave way to showbiz, and I devoted a great deal of attention to finding clubs to play in and significantly less attention to finding my way to class. I walked into one of my regular venues, Alice's Restaurant, one evening to find a young woman singing a jazz standard called "God Bless the Child" and playing a jumbo Gibson guitar that was bigger than she was. Her name was Pam Tillis, and we hit it off immediately. She had arrived at UT from Nashville, carrying a country-music pedigree as the daughter of Mel Tillis. She was already a seasoned, compelling performer and a singer who knew how to sail near the wind, delivering her lovely clear mezzo with soul and finesse. She also had a gift for harmony, and we put together a folk duo, working up a repertoire of mutually loved songs. It was Pam who first suggested I could be a professional songwriter.

The music industry was like Oz to me—mysterious and far away. I thought a person had to have a license or at least permission from the gatekeepers to write songs, and the idea that I could just start doing it was novel and thrilling. I began by imitating song structures of the popular songs I knew and used them as jumping-off places; I also relied heavily on the alternate tunings I had learned from Joni Mitchell and Crosby, Stills & Nash songbooks. Sometimes Pam would write with me, and once we collaborated on a song that her father's publishing company decided to publish and pitch to other artists. Nothing ever came of it, but the interest in something I had had a hand in writing gave me confidence that I was, indeed, a songwriter.

I was drinking almost daily and on the days when I wasn't drinking, I was eating everything I could get my hands on to recover from a hangover. I had accumulated the extra pounds known as the freshman fifteen by the end of the first semester and then another five for good measure. I also had no trouble locating cocaine providers. UT Knoxville is the size of a small town and a well-mapped territory for drug dealers in search of interested students. I was a regular customer, and the bulk of my gig money went straight up my nose. Once the drug door was open, I was receptive to trying anything at least once and became a habitual user of psychotropics such as Ecstasy and LSD, along with opiates such as quaaludes and Valium. My primary interest was in alcohol though. The drugs were enhancers that helped me stay upright and/or loose a little longer and sometimes for several days running. This combination of outside forces provided my solution, my way of tolerating myself, of feeling different and uninhibited. But my lack of inhibition led to embarrassing behavior that reinforced my self-loathing and pushed it past the tipping point where I could not stand being in my own skin without a stiff drink, and thus the cycle would begin again.

When I would inevitably crash, I would find my way back to church, confessing and renouncing my drugs of choice en route. I returned to Sequoyah Hills Presbyterian but decided that they were too forgiving, so I marched over to the Baptist Church where I expected to be held entirely accountable and submitted to full immersion in the baptismal font, hoping that the cure was in the water. These rinses would last for a week or two at the most, during which I would write to my friends in California announcing that I had found the Lord and changed my ways. They would respond with alarm and an eye-rolling dose of skepticism, suggesting that this was a temporary distraction or crutch. I would enlist my mother's help for tips on defending my faith (which should have been a tip to me that there wasn't much faith there to defend) and then beat them soundly with Bible verses. But the ink was hardly dry on the four spiritual laws before I was rolling again, a menace to myself and everyone in my path.

I received my first DUI in college, spending the night in Knoxville County Jail and lying awake listening to a group of enthusiastic women in the cells down the corridor sing spirituals through the night. My father picked me up the next morning, silent and furious—not because I was drinking and driving, not because I was drunk and driving, but because I had been mentioned in the crime beat rather than on the society page of the *Knoxville News Sentinel*. He did hire an attorney for me though, and the charge was dismissed with a fine—which he also paid, keeping my record untarnished.

If my father recognized that I was in a losing battle with substance abuse, he never said so. To him, alcohol was a foundational part of civilized living, not to mention his own world. He would occasionally pronounce his own version of the Just Say No drug campaign with: "I won't tolerate drug use. If you get into that, I'll cut you off." But he didn't pay enough attention to my activities to know much about what I was doing, and if he happened upon me in a situation that might be displeasing to him, he would keep walking.

Social standing was another thing altogether, and my father operated the command center of my activities there. The Greek culture at UT was thriving, and he insisted I go through sorority rush in my freshman year. I found this fairly excruciating, standing in a sea of girls who all knew how to do their own hair, trying to make small talk and aware that whatever I was wearing, it was wrong and, on me, matronly. I could navigate the world with a guitar and a bottle, but the disconnect between my conscious self and my femininity remained. When I was in a group of women, no matter how large or small, the inadequacy and incompatibility I felt brought out a coarseness that I couldn't control. I would swear and say inappropriate things, talk too loudly, grandstand, and ultimately, run away. A friend told me once that his therapist had advised him that the best way to live in the world was with a soft heart and a thick skin. I had it flipped; my skin was paper-thin and my heart was increasingly hard. Needless to say, I was not invited to pledge.

My social awkwardness became dysfunction in my relationships with males. I was still a virgin when I began college, a fact that I considered so condemning, so unacceptable and humiliating, that I would make up sexual escapades to talk about and look for opportunities to make it so. This should have been easy, but the young men that I targeted were similar to my father in that they were emotionally unavailable and not particularly interested in a relationship, even a fleeting one. My dating life mirrored the comedy bit "I wouldn't be a member of a club that would have me," and was thus perpetually lacking. Pam was seeing a guy named

Gus who brought a friend along one evening to make a foursome. I don't recall his name, just that he was an older man in his thirties and had a house and cocaine. He invited me to go home with him at the end of the evening and, finally, I had my chance to get high and experienced all at the same time. I found it entirely unremarkable, except for my alarm, and then shame, at the blood on his sheets. I thought I had injured myself. And I had. I had casually tossed something precious, something that was mine alone to give, to someone whose name I wouldn't even remember. Maybe there are people who can wall off their sex life from their identity and emotional stability, but I'm not one of them. Rather than being an indication of deep commitment and belonging, I used sex as a calling card, and from that time onward, threw myself at anyone who was remotely attractive to me, thinking each time that it would help my feelings of undesirability and isolation. I didn't realize the damage that I was continuing to pile up, offering myself to guys who would say things to me like: "Look, I just want to get off and pass out." I harbored ongoing fantasies of one day finding someone who would cherish me, but at that point in my life, I was under no illusions and accepted the fact that I was a means to an end. Occasionally I would actually date someone briefly, but that usually ended after some liquored-up evening where I would act out appallingly and the guy would justifiably decide I was more than he wanted to deal with.

I clung to music, still my one thing, and the only thing that brought me admiration from others. Pam and I played often in the clubs around campus and occasionally took short road trips on weekends, booking gigs in towns around East Tennessee. We were a popular act and drew crowds most shows, but even as I poured myself into each song, I continued to disrespect the gift. I smoked Marlboro reds, drank, and was high during most performances so that I could stay upright through last call. One night, at a club called the Cat's Meow, I stood up to leave with the staff, staggered, and grabbed the edge of the bar to steady myself, bringing my hand down on a pile of dirty glasses stacked up there. I cut a long gash in my right hand, severing the muscle and tendons below my thumb. A couple of the waiters took me to the hospital that was fortunately just up the street, and I had surgery that morning. The surgeon told me that I would likely not regain full use of that hand and put a cast on it, warning me that my guitar-playing days were probably over. He had no idea he had just thrown down the gauntlet. I waited until the swelling went down, pulled the cast off, and was thrashing away before the stitches were out, determined to prove him wrong. My hand stayed numb for over a year, but again, despite my every effort to ignore caring for myself, I was soon playing as before with little or no problem. I became even more brazen in my habits, dousing my boozy lifestyle in hubris, thinking I was bulletproof.

My father asked me to go through sorority rush again in the winter of my freshman year, and mostly because of my friend Andy, who convinced her Greek sisters I would be a lot of fun, I was invited to pledge Pi Beta Phi, which I did. I never overcame my feelings of estrangement around groups of women, something that remains with me to this day, but I did make a place for myself as one of the wild women in the Panhellenic community. I was a major thorn in the side of the more genteel girls who made up the sisterhood. But they tolerated me, more or less, if only as a sideshow that highlighted their own spotless purity. I began to discover, though, that among the girls who were so lovely and seemed to have such effortless lives, there were more than a few who often struggled with the same inner crises that I did. I am reminded of the saying that it is nearly always misleading and fruitless to compare my insides with another's outsides.

I remained in Knoxville over the summer, playing in clubs and working in discos as a waitress. I still could not be counted on to provide much in the way of service or hospitality, but those clubs didn't get going until ten or eleven o'clock at night, and by then, people had usually already been heavily over-served and were not particularly demanding. I could sneak drinks, too, and buy cocaine from the bartenders, which made me feel like I was friendly, alert, and on top of every detail, regardless of reality.

I found a regular job playing weeknights in the lounge at one of the local Howard Johnsons. This coincided with the arrival of a film crew who were in town shooting a movie in the foothills of the Smoky Mountains. These people were seasoned in every form of wasted living that I aspired to, and I got a thorough education during my time at HoJo's.

The bartender there was a beautiful girl named Melinda who also sold drugs; she was inexplicably found in her apartment one morning, shot in the chest. The shooting was ruled a suicide, but it was followed by several other shootings of various people of my acquaintance. One man was found in his car by the side of the road, shot gangland-style at close range in the back of the head; another bartender from one of the discos was found in similar straits.

The drug trade in Knoxville brought in a level of organized, violent crime that I had previously only been exposed to in theaters. I was oblivious, though, to the danger that surrounded me and hardly gave a thought to where I went or who I was with, repeatedly putting myself in life-threatening situations. I was driven by a single purpose—to get and stay high.

In the fall I started my sophomore year, enthusiastic only about the apartment my father had secured and furnished for me in an old Victorian house. I moved in with a kitten and my friend Patti, whom I had met the previous year and become close friends with. I declared a major in journalism, because it involved writing, but I had little or no interest in or awareness of current events, except the ones that involved me, and my love for writing did not necessarily include getting to the point. My stream-of-consciousness, self-indulgent style consistently earned me Cs and Ds, but I wasn't motivated or engaged enough to improve the situation. My attention was centered on my club life and lifestyle. Whatever small effort I put toward school was haphazard at best, and by the second semester, I was down to two classes, having missed registration due to an impromptu trip to the beach.

One of these classes was sociology, which I unexpectedly did well in because the bulk of the class was devoted to a paper we were to research and write on an aspect of sexual deviance. I spent a good bit of time in gay bars and had accumulated quite a few gay friends and acquaintances. I had a longing to decipher my father's other life that did not include me and had a tacit understanding that whatever enlightenment I would gain would not come from him. We did not speak directly about his homosexuality until nearly the end of his days, and in 1977, I think he still believed it was a secret as far as Windsor and I knew. I went to the discos, not so that I might run into him—that would have been horrible for both of us—but to somehow have closeness by association.

So when the class assignment came up, I decided to do my paper on transvestites and, in particular, drag queens, having already met a few of them in the clubs. I arranged to interview one of the more popular divas and went to his apartment over several nights after shows to record our conversations, starting at around 3:00 a.m. He immediately set me straight that he was a female impersonator, not a drag queen—the difference being that the female impersonator actually had talent and a career path, and the drag queen was merely parading around pretending to be a woman. He kept a Tom Collins glass filled, sipping it through a straw during our conversations, and spoke of how when he was Adrian, his stage name, he felt real, but when he was Steve, he didn't know who the hell he was. He would sit and talk and sip, lips and eyebrows on—perfectly painted and glossed; wig off—short, spiky hair. It was a clownish, heartbreaking picture that somehow mirrored a bit of my own experience.

I understood very well the fleeting sense of wholeness and well-being that existed in the vacuum of the stage and evaporated instantly in everyday life. I imagined that I might be able to talk with my father of the anguish of feeling like such a bad fit in the world and culture I had been born into. Surely he would understand an identity crisis as much as anyone. But he remained unwilling to participate and signaled the end of any discussion that bordered on unwelcome territory with the phrase: "Your mother and I should never have gotten divorced." From there, the conversation would migrate to galas, gossip, and fashion—frothy and safe and meaningless.

In the spring of my sophomore year, I decided that my path led somewhere other than the University of Tennessee and told my father I was dropping out of school to pursue music full-time. He didn't argue; he was aware that he was financing a party rather than an education and was glad to be relieved of the burden. I stayed in Knoxville awhile, playing in clubs and trying to save money for my next move. I thought of going to Nashville, but Pam was my only contact there, and she was living in California at the time. Nearly all my favorite bands and artists were in California, too, so I tuned my compass west again.

My father prevailed upon me to satisfy one last request before I left. I was eligible that year to be presented to society as a Knoxville debutante, and he was determined not to let the opportunity slip by. I agreed, mostly because he had just upgraded me to a little green BMW sedan, but I hadn't stopped to consider the details involved. First of all, I didn't have a date or even a candidate for a date. Secondly, although my mother had sent me to cotillion in middle school to learn ballroom dancing, I hadn't given it a thought since then and avoided dances in general. Thirdly, I would have to wear a white ball gown, and as a current size fourteen, the very idea of it brought a rush of panic.

My father suggested that his young friend Tom might be an ideal escort. I knew Tom was his boyfriend, and I was less than enthused, but I liked Tom, and he gladly stepped into his role, purchasing a tux with tails to feature his slender, lithe frame. We were enrolled, at my father's insistence, in Arthur Murray dance studio for an introductory course, and I began searching for a dress. And searching. And searching.

Thoroughly demoralized after a month or so, I finally found a pattern for a bridesmaid's formal and had it made. Even then, it pulled across my chest and flared at my waist so that everything I would have liked to hide was highlighted. I remember the moments before I was announced to a packed house at Cherokee Country Club, where my grandfather had been a board member for many years but my own father had been denied membership, due I'm sure, to his sexual orientation. Standing on the platform in an ill-fitting dress on the arm of my father's lover, who was far prettier than I was, I thought longingly of the LSD I had tucked into my evening bag for later. But I really didn't need the acid to have an out-of-body experience; I was living it.

Shortly after that, I packed up my car, drove Interstate 40 back to Barstow, and then up north to Sonoma County, returning to my mother's house, much to my stepfather's dismay.

CHAPTER SIX

· ·

THE GIFT WITH A
BEATING HEART

California

I moved back into my old bedroom in my parents' big colonial house in Petaluma and took over the lanai that was just off the living room. I established my "office" in that small, light-flooded space. It was made up mostly of windows encased in lovely old wood frames stretching from the floor to the ceiling and equally tall bookcases that required a ladder to access the top. I set up my stereo and spent most days out there, listening to music, reading the classics that my stepfather had collected, playing my guitar, and attempting to write songs. I would gaze outside at my mother's salmon-colored camellias and write ridiculous lines like: "Hiroshima was a picnic in the summertime compared to the havoc that you rendered on this heart of mine." Right. I did not know enough about relationships to fill an ad in the paper, let alone a song. I knew a great deal about longing and loneliness, but I hadn't learned to articulate that yet.

It was a brand-new day for me, though, in California. I was twenty-one and could stroll into any venue or drinking establishment, which I did regularly. I auditioned all over the Bay Area to play clubs as an opening act and started working consistently.

Most of the time, I wouldn't even make gas money, but I was playing nearly every week and meeting other musicians. Eventually I found places that booked me frequently, like the Holy City Zoo in San Francisco, a comedy club that seated around fifty people. I would warm up the crowd for improvisation groups and comedians like Dana Carvey and Bob Sarlatte, who were working out their newest bits before taking them to larger stages. I had a repertoire of cover material but nothing original of any note.

I continued to hack away nearly every day though, making up words and music, tossing the whole thing out and starting again. I had notebooks filled with ill-devised song structures and gawky lyrics, but I kept at it, mostly undeterred. When I had exhausted my thesaurus and rhyming dictionary for the day, I would beat on a set of congas, playing along to records, posturing, grandstanding—things that required little or no practice—and entertaining arena-sized dreams.

Once when my parents were away and I was babysitting Jennie and Paul, I spent the evening with my friend and neighbor Tom, whom I had known since we moved to Petaluma. He was a skate punk, childlike, and a favorite with the younger kids because of his love of play. After a few beers, the evening took a wobbly turn romantically, and we had a brief encounter that was sweet, though singular and never repeated.

The next day, I wrote my first decent song, called "King of the Court" (a nod to our cul-de-sac, Brown Court). I don't remember much beyond the first couple of lines: "He's the king of the court, all the children know. He's a lover of sport; he's a master of show."

I'm sure the lyric is in a notebook somewhere, starred repeatedly and dated, because finally I had something that conveyed real emotion with a melody that rose and fell with the feelings. I was elated. I wished Tom would park his skateboard at my front door and be my boyfriend, but I knew he had given me something far more lasting: confidence as a songwriter.

As I got to know other musicians in the area, I started to play in duos, trios, and eventually bands. I played often with my friends Nina and Kim. I met other artists in the area who had successful, working bands and offered me opportunities. I joined my friend Sarah's group as a backup singer. She was from Memphis and one of the biggest acts in Sonoma County. I was excited to be a part of a high-profile band and worked night and day learning the parts. I had them down cold, but when showtime rolled around, my performances were tainted and ultimately sabotaged by alcohol and drug use, and I would wind up snorting cocaine and drinking to incapacity. Ultimately Sarah fired me, a recurring theme in my interaction with other musicians. She kindly spoke to me about my obvious substance-abuse problem, but I could not hear it. Not then. I rationalized that she drank and used drugs herself, so who was she to comment about my habits?

I vowed to practice self-control and pressed on. I booked shows in Ukiah and Mendocino and would spend weekends playing various clubs. Friday night would begin well enough, but someone would emerge from the backwoods, cocaine in hand, and Friday would bleed into Saturday and then Sunday, when I would spend the drive back to Petaluma trying to piece the weekend together or forget it entirely. I would resolve anew and book a show at a family-friendly pizza parlor nearby, after which I would be unable to pass up Red's Recovery Room on my way home, a dive bar where absolutely no one was recovering, and start the wheel spinning again.

Once as I was leaving San Francisco drunk in the early hours of the morning, I ran a red light and hit another car in the intersection. I didn't stop but continued on, driving in circles around Golden Gate Park to make sure I wasn't followed. To this day I don't know if anyone in the other car was injured or the extent of the damage. My car had only a slight dent. I thought about it briefly and remorsefully the next morning and then put it out of my mind and memory entirely, tossing it on the overgrown pile of shameful, out-of-control conduct. I did not recall the incident until more than thirty years later sitting in an AA meeting. I was listening to someone else's tale of a hit-and-run with no idea of the outcome and suddenly thought: *I did that too.*

I did my best to hide my behavior from my mother and stepfather, but it was impossible for them to miss. They insisted that I attend church while under their roof, and my mother would tersely whisper to me nearly every Sunday that I smelled like a liquor cabinet as I sat next to her in the pew sweating fumes and trying to stay awake. Eventually, my stepfather said I needed to find my own place to live.

I wasn't making enough money gigging to pay living expenses, so I started looking for a job and a rental to move to. My cousin Neel had come to California several years previously and was living and working in San Francisco. She didn't like her apartment and wanted to get out of the city, but she was leery about throwing her lot in with me. She liked her wine but also her solitude and had an uneasy sense that my drinking habits and activities fell into a different category than hers. I found the solution to her objections in a perfect little two-bedroom dollhouse in Petaluma, and though she could easily resist me, she couldn't resist such a charming address. We got along well most of the time, and she became as a sister to me.

She joined a vanpool and commuted to the city to her job at the Bank of California. She had been working a second job part-time at a commodity brokerage firm and got me a job there, too, working as an assistant. The brokers were trained salesmen who knew little or nothing about futures trading and were instructed to follow the printouts from the parent company in Boston when making recommendations to their clients. But nearly all of them were going rogue. They were making a killing in commissions and credited their own opinions and strategies, which were usually quickened and punctuated by stimulants and pot-laced with PCP. My unhappy task was to make the inevitable calls to clients about market losses. I hated the job, but I loved the party atmosphere in the office. It was no different than the bars I frequented. After work I would ride the express bus back to Petaluma, usually sleeping off the day's activities or sitting in the midst of paranoid delusions and dread for fifty minutes nonstop.

In the evenings, Neel and I bought gallon jugs of Napa County wine and floated checks at South City Market down the street, where the owners, Ralph and Helen, knew us by name and treated us like their wayward children. Neel would watch television in her room while I sat at the kitchen table piecing together songs, a tumbler of wine at my fingertips, a Marlboro burning in the ashtray, squeezing as much romance as I could out of the fantasy that these, like pencil and paper, were the tools of the writer.

My father sent the furniture he had supplied for my apartment in Knoxville, and we used my grandmother's china, bought more furniture, and filled the front window boxes with geraniums and vinca vines. We loved our little home and contributed equally to maintaining it inside and out. We put sod in the back garden and adopted puppies that promptly tore up the sod. We met our neighbors and pursued respectability.

Neel was a homebody for the most part, but occasionally I would talk her into some escapade or another, like going to a Christmas tree farm to cut down our own tree. We had already repeatedly over-served ourselves and went careening to the farm where we picked out a tree that was barely five feet tall. Regardless, neither one of us was in any shape to chop it down, drag it to the car, and tie it on the roof. But Neel's people skills were as thick as her Southern accent, and she peeled back the drape of her wraparound skirt, exposing her well-turned ankles, and easily charmed a young man into securing the tree—but not her phone number, as I'm sure he was hoping. We pitched and lurched our way back home to more wine and an evening of decorating and Christmas music, laughing about our reckless afternoon.

And truly, there were times of hilarity that reinforced my thinking that a life without a drink was a dreary life indeed. But in the midst of all the freewheeling remained the thread of despair that would weave itself into a blanket in the early hours before dawn. I would sit in a rocking chair in the living room, alone, too drunk to function, too coked up to sleep, knowing that there was precious little that was zany and fun-filled regarding my drinking habits and trying to silence the judge and jury in my head with defeated prayers that didn't amount to much more than: "I'm sorry, I'm sorry, I'm sorry." I was like a cornered child trying to fend off a beating from a raging father. There was a part of me that wanted the beating though, wanted it to kill me.

My friend Laurel and her husband, Dale, had moved to Petaluma, and I spent a lot of time with them. There was always beer in their refrigerator, and they were hardly prudish about drinking, but Laurel also challenged me about my Christianity. She had taken me to Young Life camps when I was a teenager and she was a leader. She knew I had made more than one profession of faith in those days, and she could see that I was sprawling in chaos with a head full of Bible verses—particularly the ones involving warnings—and a résumé of bad behavior. She urged me to go to church with them, a charming little Episcopal church. The nave was like a jewel box, and I loved the beauty of it and the quiet reverence that permeated the space. It was restful to me, though I found the services tedious in length. I was accustomed to Presbyterian services, which set their watches at exactly one hour, and chafed at the repetition of the Common Book of Prayer and the extra thirty minutes devoted to communion. But truthfully, no church, no service, no liturgy was going to work for me at that point. At best it was distant poetry, a song intended for someone else; at worst, condemning. I did not believe in a God who was for me; I believed in a God who was furious with me.

I knew very little about addiction as an illness and even less about recovery. I had heard of AA but thought it was a group of homeless people and ex-convicts who got together in warehouses to smoke cigarettes and one-up each other with their drunk-a-logues. I believed my substance-abuse issues were simply sins that needed repentance, and that all would be remedied if I could only learn some restraint. On the rare occasions when I peeled back the edge of the lid on my own denial (or had it done for me by a well-meaning friend or family member) and realized that I had lost the ability to control my drug and alcohol use—if I had ever had it in the first place—I would attend prayer services and go forward for deliverance at the altar calls.

Occasionally I would have a brief period of sobriety. I would begin to feel a tiny spark of hope; I would clean the house, swim laps in my friend Constance's pool, and start a diet. I would offer a few tentative prayers. I would call my mother, confess everything (very bad idea), and tell her that I was turning a corner, that I could feel it. Then on an ordinary weeknight, I would find that I could not sit still, that my skin prickled and tingled, that I could not bear my own company, and I would be out the door, heading to downtown Petaluma or down the street to the drug dealer's house. I would more than make up for my time away and stay out until every place was closed and every light was off. Then I would blearily look for someone who might be continuing the party at home and carry on until the sun came up and I was crawling into bed with a man whom I may have just met thirty minutes previously.

My second DUI came on one of those nights. I lived less than two miles from where I had parked. I was driving my mother's station wagon, having recently wrecked my BMW, and managed to sideswipe an entire line of parked cars as I drove. The station wagon was stuttering and gasping, but I willed it on, another hit-and-run, and finally got it into my front yard where it collapsed, totaled. The police simply followed the trail of radiator fluid to my house, and while Neel stood in the front yard gaping, they tossed me in the back of the squad car and took me to jail. The Petaluma Police Department was a fairly docile place, and I crashed on a cot in a single cell and passed out. I walked home the next morning preparing to face my parents' wrath, which greeted me at the front door in the form of hopeless resignation. They said they would take the BMW, which had only needed minor repairs, and sell it to replace my mother's car. They said they didn't know what it was going to take with me but that eventually I would have to answer to God. Now without wheels, I walked down the street to see my friend and late-night companion Leroy, who happened to be an attorney, and asked him to represent me in court. He got me off with a fine and probation. I scraped together $400 and bought a little Fiat sedan. I don't remember whether I lost my insurance over it or what happened with the other cars involved; my father had continued to pay for my coverage, and I left it for him to deal with. The privileged life that I led with access to finances and favors afforded me another slap on the wrist and this incident, much like the others, became part of the trail behind me. I continued on, just as before, for several more years. I covered the territory from south of San Francisco to northern Ukiah in search of a gig or a party and usually found both.

I continued working on songs, writing and rewriting lyrics, experimenting with guitar tunings, and over time began to accumulate a handful of songs that were genuinely distinctive and well written. I was gradually finding my voice as an artist and used that to bolster my denial. I couldn't be that far gone if I was able to write good music. I found many great musicians to play with who saw something valuable in me as an artist but also saw the tremendous liability of getting involved with me professionally. I was an expert in self-sabotage, regularly doing things like booking a well-paying band date at a winery, which could have led to regular work, and then dropping LSD the night of the show, consuming copious amounts of wine, crashing backward into the drum set laughing maniacally, and leaving without a paycheck as the manager sputtered in rage.

Ultimately I also lost my job at the commodity brokerage house, which took some doing in that crowd. But Neel came through for me once more, landing me a job as an account assistant at the Bank of California, and I continued to commute to San Francisco, working weekdays and playing clubs on the weekends. BankCal was a far more conservative environment, but the job was fairly easy. I opened and closed checking and savings accounts and made sure the signature card made it into the right file. I was a marginal employee, but I put forth a small effort, because I was grateful for the paycheck and the health insurance.

At a party in Petaluma, I met a guy who had a large stash of cocaine that he freely carved into rails, striping the mirror on the coffee table. He latched on to me, chattering away about his life and his theories about life with the stuttering untempered surge of thought that is the common exchange among drug abusers. But I recognized a gravy train when I saw one and happily listened to his conversational nonsense in exchange for unlimited access to his blow, and by sunup I had a steady boyfriend. His name was Rick, and he had a long-term job doing trim work on the buildings that dotted George Lucas's Industrial Light & Magic compound in San Marin. At that point he had been working on the property for several years and had a nice house in Petaluma, and initially I thought I had hit the lottery. Rick was handsome, generous with his drugs, and in many ways well-meaning. But the substance of the relationship was contained in a tiny glass vial, and we had absolutely nothing in common beyond that. After less than a month, we both realized that there wasn't enough cocaine anywhere to make us compatible, although, ever attentive to my own interests, I stuck around long enough to attend the Industrial Light & Magic Christmas party that was held in San Francisco that December. That was it. Except it wasn't it. I discovered several weeks later that I was pregnant.

I fell into a new low of apprehension and dread. I genuinely believed that the worst had come upon me and that this event marked the beginning of the end. My neighbor and friend, Joanie, brought over pamphlets from the crisis pregnancy center where she worked, and I read about the embryo as an individual life with a beating heart and brain waves that was probably already sucking its uniquely printed thumb in my womb. I read about the horror of various current termination methods, such as vacuuming, and the irreparable physical and emotional damage that I would do to myself if I were to abort.

The pamphlet was designed to appeal to everything maternal in me, but it was unnecessary. I wouldn't have aborted the baby. But not because I trusted God or thought that He would help me—far from it. And it was not because I held any deep convictions, spiritually, morally, politically, or otherwise. I simply was too broken and too terrified to do anything but accept my lot, even though I had no idea how I was going to manage. I could not even stay sober for a month, let alone nine of them. I assumed that I would fail at pregnancy just as I had at every other aspect of my life and that God's righteous punishment for my crimes, the bitter end I had been fully expecting all along, would be a baby with birth defects, a living testament to my own wretchedness.

My family accepted the news with the air of weary inevitability that had become part and parcel of my stream of bad tidings. But my mother felt strongly about Right to Life issues and, in spite of her own justified concerns, offered her support and encouragement, which I deeply appreciated. My father's response was disappointment, which I expected, but also kindness, which I did not expect. Neel and my friends drew near and offered help.

The only one who wanted nothing to do with any of it was Rick. I went to see him and told him the situation. He responded by questioning whether or not the baby was his, which was a legitimate concern, but I was sure—not because of any faithfulness on my part but because of a lack of other opportunities. Then he said he would pay for an abortion, but he didn't want any part of bringing a baby into the aftermath of a failed relationship. Frankly, I was relieved. I was already overwhelmed and didn't want to have to deal with another opinion, so I quickly told him he was off the hook in every way and then asked if I could have access to medical records if I needed them. We did not speak again for a long, long while.

I went back to St. Johns, the little Episcopal church, and was greeted with compassion and practical help. Women, young and old, rallied around me, and I began to feel a bit stronger. I became determined to have a clean pregnancy and started walking every day and trying to eat well. My health insurance with BankCal had cleared just a couple of weeks before my conception, and I was elated to find that I had a policy that paid for everything, with the exception of a small co-pay. I wondered if maybe that was a gift from God.

Emotionally I would swing wildly from my initial dread to thinking that maybe I could be a mother to inquiring with private adoption agencies, wanting a situation far more stable than anything I could provide for my baby. I had no idea where I was going; I got out of bed every morning and held on to whatever was in front of me.

But then there were slips—an innocuous little word for lost weekends where I would fall back into drinking and using, causing even the most hardened drug dealers to refuse to cater to me when I showed up at their doors in maternity clothes and an obvious baby bump. I found a way though, and the remorse and desolation that followed were lower than any place I had been before.

I had long since stopped caring much about my own well-being, but the knowledge that someone else, someone defenseless with no say in the matter, was involved was crushing to me and confirmed every bit of disgust I had ever felt about myself—and then some. I would crawl up out of the shame and white-knuckle my way through another couple of months before it happened again.

Once I called my mother to tell her of my latest relapse, and she became enraged, reminding me that Jesus said in every gospel but one that anyone who harmed a child would do better with a millstone tied around their neck and tossed in the sea than to face the punishment that awaited them. I knew she was trying to protect the baby, I knew I had been seeking this kind of response calling her in the first place, I knew I needed help, but I didn't know where to get it—and at that point, neither did she. In 1982, addiction-treatment centers were hardly on the horizon, let alone part of the public lexicon, and even if they had been, I don't know that I would have considered myself a candidate. I was convinced it was a moral failure. But it was a moral failure I was powerless to overcome. I began to cry out to God in a way that I had not done before, as an advocate for the baby, which made me bolder.

I questioned His integrity entrusting a life to me. I did not expect Him to help me for my sake, but I asked Him to help me stay sober, to help me find a loving adoptive family, to help me, please, just help me.

In the midst of this, I began to feel the baby move, and with each little somersault in my womb, my heart responded. For the first time in my life I belonged to someone and someone belonged to me. I realized that this wasn't just a baby. It was my baby. I did everything I could to keep myself from drinking and using— which mostly meant switching to food, which, in this instance, was acceptable to me. Still, there were moments when my resolve caved in, and I was at the bar again, unable to stay away. Finally, in my last trimester, the urge to pick up lifted, and I was able to finish my pregnancy sober.

With every kick and flutter, though, it became obvious to me that whatever happened, it was not in me to give my baby up. That little heartbeat was the only thing keeping me tied to the planet, the only thing that gave me any desire for a future. Toward the end of my pregnancy, I told my mother that I would keep the baby, fully expecting her to challenge my decision and remind me that I was the poorest of choices for motherhood, but to my surprise she tearfully said that she wanted that too. She became even more supportive, coming over to walk with me, attending Lamaze classes with me, helping plan a massive baby shower with my friends that supplied nearly everything I needed and, most importantly, giving me a feeling of courage and hope with her own implacable optimism and faith.

In September of 1982, I began to have contractions and went into labor two weeks after my due date. In California, natural childbirth was a badge of honor that everyone I knew wore proudly, and though I had never waited to discover my pain tolerance before killing it with one thing or another, my intent was to join the ranks of all the brave women who had gone before me.

But labor was like having an internal expander installed in my uterus, cranking it quickly from zero to ten, letting it collapse, and cranking again every five minutes until every bone, every muscle, every bit of sinew felt close to snapping. I can't say I behaved nobly; I can't say much about it at all except I stayed with it for fourteen hours, after which my doctor did an exam and told me my baby was breech and I would need a cesarean section. I was relieved to know that I would be getting painkillers under a doctor's orders, excited and extremely fearful about my child's condition all at the same time.

The C-section was fairly quick and unremarkable. I was sedated but awake and have a blurry memory of a tiny infant brought close before I was taken to recovery. My mother met me there and exclaimed: "I have seen her, and she is gorgeous!" I quickly asked her if everything was all right—implicitly and even expectantly wondering about defects. "No, no, no," she said. "All is well."

I fell asleep for a couple of hours, and when I woke, a nurse brought my daughter to me, bundled in a pink blanket and wearing a little cap that I lifted to find a Mohawk of blonde curls. She was perfect. She was beautiful and perfect. I named her Rebecca Neel. And in that moment, I had my first recognized encounter with God as I know Him today. It was as if He pulled back an invisible curtain and said to me: "See, I'm not who you think I am."

In those days, women who had cesarean sections stayed in the hospital for a week. A week. A week during which I learned to nurse, to swaddle, to bathe, and burp—all the practical points of caring for my daughter—from the maternity-ward staff who were intent on sending me off with as much confidence as they could quickly build in me. All the while, I felt the presence of Jesus in my hospital room. He didn't tell me anything. He didn't ask me anything. He just sat with me. I didn't really know how to frame this experience, but I knew that it was very, very different from the God of my understanding. I expected judgment. I encountered tenderness and mercy. Something inside of me began to tentatively open and flower. I thought maybe I could live.

My mother and stepfather graciously invited us to stay with them while I recovered from my surgery, and for three weeks, we set up camp in my old bedroom. I put Rebecca in a bassinet by my bed and responded to her every cry or chirp with increasing recognition of her needs and ease in my role. My mother was attentive and helpful, which was a great comfort to me and not altogether unexpected.

My father's behavior, on the other hand, was entirely shocking. He carried the initial infant photos of a scrunched little face looking slightly alarmed in his wallet, showing them to everyone he encountered and proclaiming that he was a grandfather. I don't know how he sidestepped the questions regarding my marriage—or lack of one. I would guess that he simply did what he usually did with questions that he disliked and ignored them. I suspect there was a piece of defiance relating to his own unorthodox and socially detested lifestyle in his celebratory attitude, but a friend of his told me once that he would produce the pictures with a flourish, silently daring anyone to say an unkind word.

He arrived with boxes of baby clothes from Neiman Marcus and pronounced Rebecca a beauty. He told me that she should call him Grandpapa, with an accent on the second syllable. Ultimately it came out sounding more like Grand Poobah, but it didn't matter. He was "Papa" and a devoted one at that. He loved Rebecca without reservation and never wavered in his affection. He told me that I didn't have to go back to my bank job when my leave was up and that he would help me indefinitely so I could stay home with her. I felt utterly relieved.

Motherhood gave me a sense of purpose and identity, and I assumed it would supply the cure for overcoming my excesses. I had the want-to, but I lacked the how-to, and I clung to my long-cherished notion that moderation was the key, inevitably popping the cork or flipping the top. It would start with: "Just a glass of wine." But then I would find my way to the end of the bottle, pack my baby in a Snugli, walk down the street to the cocaine dealer's house, put her on a bed in the back room, and wade into oblivion until sometime after daylight. Once, our host became angry over some perceived slight and shot a handgun at the wall. I thought of my sleeping child in the next room and how easily she could have been in the path of that bullet. I let the horror of my reality touch me briefly, but only long enough to determine plan number 1001, in which I would effectively overcome my weakness once and for all.

Gradually these incidents increased, and I would ask my mom to keep Becca for the weekend so I could go and play gigs. Two nights of playing were corseted with a twenty-four-hour party in between, and I would show up, sleepless and obviously unhinged, to get my baby. I tried my same remedies again: going to church, sticking with steadier friends, and eating until I was sick. I thought often of the encounter I had had with God in the hospital. I knew it was real, and yet there was not a shred of evidence that anything was remotely different in my life. Every dry stretch was followed by a deeper plunge off the wagon, and finally, late in the spring, my stepfather, reading the writing that blazed across the sky and foretold a future where he and my mother would be raising their granddaughter, called and asked for a meeting. He told me that my mom was too wrapped up in my life, that she had her own life, and that I needed to pull myself together, grow up, and get on with it. Then in a fairly bold move, he ordered me to leave the state of California. In an equally surprising move, I agreed.

I was ready for a change, and as before, the geographical cure contained irresistible promise to me for a do-over. It did not occur to me to examine the fact that my previous episodes of bouncing back and forth had never brought me any success in overcoming my drug and alcohol issues. But I recognized that I couldn't make a life or a living playing in clubs and that the only thing I had any remote possibility of a career in was music. I didn't have the courage or the means to go to Los Angeles or New York, but Tennessee was home to me. I had a loose plan of returning to Knoxville, getting a job, saving money, and eventually relocating to Nashville. That was it. I had no idea what I would do once I was in Nashville. I simply marked it as my goal, assuming that I would make a place for myself. My father was happy to have Rebecca closer to him and agreed to help me move. Neel had fallen in love with one of the senior vice presidents at BankCal and was planning her marriage. It seemed that every circumstance was a sign that this chapter in California was finishing its last sentence.

CHAPTER SEVEN

....

GEOGRAPHY, SELF-CONTROL, AND ALL THE CURES THAT AREN'T

Tennessee

In the summer of 1983, I packed up and left Petaluma for Knoxville, hopeful of building a life with my daughter and sure that the change of address would provide the stability I was lacking. My father gave me a job at his design firm doing menial work, pulling discontinued fabrics and wallpaper samples. I was a marginal, unnecessary employee, but it was a way to put me on the payroll and provide me with health insurance without looking like he was supporting me. He was quick to rescue me, equally quick to resent it, and every check he ever wrote to me came at an unspoken price. But I was willing to tolerate his disappointed silences in exchange for a salary. I had been doing that unofficially for years anyway.

My sister Windsor was finishing school and agreed to an apartment together. We found a townhouse we loved, and our father happily set about decorating it, indulging his baseless fantasy of his young ingenue daughters stepping into their fashionable adult lives. He finished in time for Becca's first birthday and called for a party that included several of his friends and not a single child. He was utterly doting though, and Becca was wild about him.

My high school and college friends were nearly all married, which gave me an opportunity to keep a fairly low profile, another scheme for staying sober. I didn't play in clubs much; I worked during the day and stayed home most nights, although I did find a handful of musicians to collaborate with occasionally.

But eventually, inevitably, I started dipping into wine after I put Becca to bed and found it was easy and, in some ways preferable, to drink alone. I could fully indulge my dreams of an unlimited future, talk to the television, and pour away while ironing one of Becca's lacy, petticoated dresses, courtesy of Papa, or sitting at the kitchen table piecing together a song.

I could also rationalize my loss of resolve: I wasn't hurting anyone, just unwinding after work, like everybody else. I would mentally recite all the people in my life who were stable, productive citizens and also enjoyed an occasional cocktail, including my sister. But Windsor was not a drinker, and although I'm sure she was aware of my problem and most likely alarmed, I don't remember her saying much about it. I do remember that she was kind and helpful to me with Becca. We had been at odds throughout our childhood, competing and fighting regularly and sometimes viciously, but much of the discord that existed between us melted during our time together in Knoxville.

I reconnected with Pam Tillis, who was living in a little house in Nashville with her son, Ben, and she invited me to come for a visit one weekend. We had a fine time catching up, and she drove me around the neighborhood known as Music Row on a short tour of the city. Here was the Warner Bros. building, there was CBS, RCA, and MCA. No gates, no guards—here was the industry I longed to be part of, clustered at random in shabby old houses and newer construction over three long streets. I had no idea how the business itself worked. Three cassette recordings—one by Emmy Lou Harris, one by Rodney Crowell, and one by Roseanne Cash—were the extent of my knowledge of country music. I also didn't realize that Nashville was a songwriter's town, that many of the little houses up and down 16th and 17th Avenues were publishers. It was hardly a grand picture but still exciting and mysterious to me.

At night, we went to clubs to see Pam's favorite bands. On the way to one show, she talked up the guitar player, someone named Kenny Greenberg. She said: "You have to hear this guy play. It's unreal, like he's telling a complete story in his solos. And it's a story you feel like you know, because you relate to the emotional content, but there's always a surprise too."

We met Kenny on his birthday, December 9. He was eating a handful of M&Ms between sets and wearing a button-down shirt with the sleeves torn off and a black beret. Not that I remember.

Pam told me that if I wanted to move to Nashville, there was an extra bedroom in her house that Becca and I could have. I returned to Knoxville lit up with intention and purpose. The idea that I could live in a music community, that I could be with a majority who were like me rather than the token party favor in a white-collar crowd ("Ashley, bring your guitar and play us a song!") was a firecracker of motivation. I socked my paychecks away, wrote song after song, and organized a demo session with local musicians to get some current material on tape. I hoped to find a record deal;

I needed to find a life. No matter that at the time Nashville wasn't much of a rock 'n' roll town; it was a music town, and it was in Tennessee, which was home.

I told myself, again, that my drinking issues were environmental and circumstantial. I drank because I was a misfit; I drank because I was lonely; I drank because my job wasn't the least bit engaging or satisfying; I drank to pass the time until I could step into my real life. On it went. Denial comes in many forms: pretending something doesn't exist, minimizing, blaming, excusing, generalizing, dodging, attacking, and so forth. I was never far from a very good reason to justify my drinking. So I drank. But I was convinced that once I crossed the Davidson County line into Nashville I would be someone different. And that person would be a moderate social drinker who was too busy as an artist of interest to drink herself into a nightly stupor.

On August 1, 1984, I left Knoxville with Becca and drove across the Cumberland Plateau to the place that truck drivers call the Guitar Town. My father sent a van with my furniture, and I set up our space in a bedroom in Pam's house on Branch Creek Road. Initially I drove around the city, trying to get my bearings. I had absolutely nothing happening for a long while, but I had an overwhelming sense that I was in the right place and that was enough.

Sometime during the next few months, I met a publisher, Don Gant, who liked my songs and began working with me. I played writers' nights at places like the Bluebird Cafe and took my demo tapes around to get work singing. Initially, most of my efforts never went anywhere. Once I got a call to sing in a background vocal section on a jingle. I showed up and the engineer looked at me blankly. When I told him my name, he laughed and said: "Oh, we thought you were a man." Turns out the tape I'd sent was defective and running slow. They thought they'd hired a bass singer.

Gradually I began to meet people through Pam and through Don, who footed the bill for a demo session on a handful of songs. The session turned out well and delivered me a little local notice. I took full advantage of Pam's babysitter list and was out nearly every night in clubs, meeting, greeting, asking to sit in, and drinking. Whatever triumphant idea I may have had of overcoming my habit disappeared into the wild crowd I located and made a heat-seeking beeline for.

My mother urged me to find a church. I found a Presbyterian congregation that was similar to the ones I had grown up in and started attending on Sundays if I wasn't too hungover. I thought about God, probably daily. My experience of Him bending down into my hospital room had faded, but I knew it was real and still carried a tiny jewel with me from that encounter: the knowledge that He loved me. I didn't have the slightest idea why, and I thought that surely by now He had changed His mind in light of the obvious fact that I was the same dissolute person. I felt bewildered by it all: How could such a profound experience leave me virtually untouched? Or had it?

Having Becca had given me a desire and framework for responsibility that was stronger than anything I'd had before, but as previously noted, it hadn't gotten me sober. Once I got to

Nashville, it took no time at all for me to fall back into binge drinking, cocaine abuse, and promiscuity. I had fewer opportunities, but I indulged them fully. I had landed in an artistic community where nearly everyone I met was in the middle of creating their own depraved story, so I added "Everybody's doing it" to my denial list and carried on. The duality of my life was not lost on me, though, and I had many voices in my head, most of them making accusations. I knew I wasn't going to be able to maintain the charade of being dressed up on Sunday and drunk on Monday indefinitely. I just didn't know where the pendulum would rest when it finally stopped swinging. I wrote songs about faith or the idea of it or the longing for it. I wrote songs about love, the lack of it. I joked that my songs were a catalog of despair with an occasional bit of hope in the refrains. I did not like to sit still very long unless I was loaded, lost in the music, or both.

I met an artist named Gene Cotton, who was successfully working the NACA circuit, an acronym for the National Association of Campus Activities. A lot of colleges would parse out their entertainment budgets over the course of the school year on unknown or lesser-known acts, rather than big stars, in order to stretch the dollars. Gene kindly introduced me to his agent, and I began getting work at campuses throughout the region playing student events. I would get up in the middle of the night and drive to a school where I would play that night and drive home the next day. It was a better paycheck than any club gig I had ever had and gave me some optimism that I could eventually find financial independence from my father.

I planned a trip back to California for Christmas. Late in the fall, my mother called to tell me that their garage had caught fire and burned. I had stored a large number of boxes in the attic of the garage, including some with valuable china and silver belonging to my grandmother. When I arrived in California, my mother gave me a sizable insurance check for the loss, and I immediately cashed it and contacted the nearest cocaine dealer. The visit was a blur. My sister and my father had both come for the holiday as well, so I had plenty of willing babysitters. Claiming that I needed to reconnect with old friends, I stayed up and out every night. I was using around the clock so I could care for Becca during the day and pretend nothing was out of the ordinary. I was utterly blind to my condition but I was the only one. Everyone in my family was on red alert to the truth of my illness and the potential, inevitable destruction for me and for my child. On the day of our departure back to Tennessee, my sister came into my room while I was packing.

The Big Book of Alcoholics Anonymous advises that when confronting an addict, it's important to be calm and unemotional, to stick to the facts and avoid accusing or attacking. Windsor hadn't read the Big Book. She was thinking about Rebecca, whom she loved dearly; she was thinking about me, too. She became hysterical to near incoherence and said simply: "If you don't get help, you will die, and Becca won't have a father or a mother."

I had a month's worth of dates booked and told her I didn't have time to go to the hospital. She shouted at me that I was crazy, that none of that work mattered, because it wouldn't last anyway if

I kept on like this. She said if I would stay in California and go for treatment, she would stay too and take care of Becca. I stood there, watching her sobbing, and something in me broke. I said okay. I knew I couldn't continue as I was and survive, but I didn't feel relief; I felt beaten. I thought, even then: *I don't think I want to live without a drink.* But I did want to try for Becca's sake. I wanted to know that I had done everything within my power on her behalf. The problem was, I didn't have any power. I was out of control in every area of my life. I didn't realize that in acknowledging that, I had just passed Go.

My stepfather specialized in hospital law and was the attorney for Petaluma Valley Hospital, which had recently installed an addiction-treatment unit in an unused wing. Within the week I was admitted, escorted by both my parents. They walked me to my room and said their good-byes, my father weeping and my mother brimming with assurances of success. I don't remember much about the first few days except for the comfort I felt every time an orderly came by with the candy cart. I stayed for a month and I began to get an education about the disease of alcoholism. I tentatively examined the truth of my life and condition, pulling each delusion from the tangle, strand by strand. I mourned the loss of wine at dinner. Gradually I admitted to myself that I would never interfere with a good buzz by introducing food, and that the wine *was* my dinner. I thought of every happy, funny, carefree moment I had ever had while drinking and believed that the life ahead of me was sure to be filled with austerity and doldrums.

As time went on, though, I encountered something I'd long forgotten: peace. I recognized that I was in a secure place, far from the daily realities, and that soon enough I would have to return and face them, but for now, my world was made up of a small group of people who were in the same shape as me and a clean, slightly antiseptic environment that felt curative. I became willing to look at how much of my time as an addict was spent in desolation compared with the brief moments of gaiety. I looked at my repeated, failed attempts at mastering my drinking and using. I understood that I did not have the ability to free myself. I did the twelve-step work sheets on steps one, two, and three. I turned my life and my will over to the Lord's care. I wondered if I meant it.

I later saw a few pictures of myself during my hospital stay, moon-faced and disheveled, but there was also an absence of tension in those photos and in a couple of them I was actually relaxed and smiling.

I wished I could stay longer.

I left the treatment center promising to stay in touch with my fellow patients, excited to be reunited with Becca, and anxious about returning to Tennessee. Sugar was my current panacea, and I had gained about ten pounds in the hospital. But I wasn't sure there was enough ice cream and candy in Nashville to help me stay clean and sober. When we returned home, Pam said we hadn't missed anything except a major snowstorm that paralyzed the city for a week. Apparently a lot of us had been brought to a standstill that January.

I returned to my publisher's office and announced that I was now in recovery and would no longer be participating in the ongoing parties. They all said they were impressed and wished they could be that strong and "Good on ya." I cleaned my room and started rebooking the dates I had canceled. I felt focused and useful. Then the weekend rolled around, and I had a Friday night with nothing to do. I went over to see my friend James and told him about treatment. He kept saying: "You mean, you can never drink again?" "Not even once?" "Don't they teach you how to control it?"

I said: "No, I can never drink again."

I said: "Well, maybe once."

I said: "What are you drinking?"

I hardly skipped a beat before I had a beer, then two, then I was out the door for a six-pack. I drank all night long. The next day, I had to drive to Knoxville for an event with my father, and I spent the next three hours navigating Interstate 40 with a pounding head. I drove through Cookeville and Crossville, wailing and shouting over and over again: "I am not going to live like this one more day. Not one more day." And there it was, like manna, like quail, the gift that becomes the gateway: willingness.

CHAPTER EIGHT

SURRENDER, PART ONE

Tennessee

I found an AA meeting before I left Knoxville and at the end of the
meeting went forward to receive the silver chip that is also called
the Desire Chip, indicating the crossroad to choosing a new way
of life. I returned to Nashville and started attending meetings. I
hated them. Walking into a group of strangers put me right back
in elementary school, though I didn't understand it at the time. I
wanted to go, I needed to go, but I could hardly make myself go.
When I did manage to attend a meeting, I would search my mind
for something lucid or funny or inspiring or simply true to say. I
would fight past a protesting stomach to speak up, but the minute
I started talking, my ears would pound, and I would complete
less than half of my initial thought before eventually trailing off,
like a toy that had wound down. After the meeting I would chide
myself out the door and all the way home: "You idiot—you sound
insane." "Just sit there and be quiet." "Stop trying so hard." "You
don't have anything to say," and so on. I would ask someone to
sponsor me and then avoid calling her. My meeting attendance
gradually went from sporadic to unusual to nil. I decided I would
stay sober on my own terms and I did—for a while.

I went back to church and met with the assistant pastor. I told him that I was recently out of treatment, that my sobriety had already suffered a setback. I asked if there was something there I could become part of, someplace I could try to fit in. He said there was a Sunday-evening service that hadn't really gotten off the ground and was quite small. He thought I could help build it up by supplying some music and maybe it would help me too. I agreed. I started going regularly and found a society of fellow mavericks who encouraged me in life and faith. I found that playing and singing hymns and spirituals eased the turbulence in my head and heart like no other music.

I read the Bible and went to the women's Bible study, encountering more friendships there. I discovered women of all ages who felt as alienated and lacking in confidence as I did. There were women with crippling secrets, women overcome with the cares of the world, women who didn't think they mattered one way or the other and who had disappeared into the lives of their husband and children, leaving little trace of themselves. I loved them all and the church became an umbrella of support to me.

One month when I found I couldn't meet my rent, I went to the elders and asked for help. They asked what I did for a living, and I said that I sang on recordings and performed, mostly in bars. I said that I had come to Nashville to eventually get a record deal and become famous. They looked at me and at one another. They wrote the check without another word. Occasionally I would also receive checks in the mail from various church members, whom I slightly knew or didn't know at all, saying they had been thinking of me. I thought of these events as God on the ground, stretching out His hand, wiggling His fingers, saying hello.

My friend Wally introduced me to a therapist who was starting a group for musicians. Everyone in the group was either an addict or a co-addict, and I managed to make a place for myself there too. I met people inside and outside the AA rooms who had recently started recovery and began pursuing friendships; I fared far better one-on-one.

Gradually I found some kind of footing, although the first few months of sobriety were a daily struggle, and I couldn't imagine that I would ever be a whole person. I mourned the loss of alcohol like a cherished friend, but I had expected that giving it up would signal an end to my problems. Now I was in the wilderness of realizing that I couldn't live with it, and I couldn't live without it, and truly, my problems were just getting under way. I was overwhelmed with unchecked feelings that rose up and crashed over me in rolling swells. But I discovered I could mentally tune into a white noise frequency, similar to a "sound soother," and I spent a large part of my time there for some emotional relief.

After my third car wreck while in that vacated state, I received a letter from the Tennessee Department of Safety declaring me a liability and threatening to revoke my license permanently if there were any more incidents.

I peeked out of my fog. I found an apartment and "acted as if": acted as if I were a functioning member of society, acted as if I were a confident parent, acted as if I knew what I was doing in the recording studio, acted as if I knew what I was doing anywhere.

I enrolled Becca in preschool. I stepped up my therapy and added individual sessions to the group experiences. I continued to find work as a singer and gradually began singing background on albums in nearly every musical genre. I got another publishing deal that actually paid an advance on salary. I put together one band and then another. I played showcases. I took meetings. I read the *Big Book* and started working on a fourth-step inventory. I was nothing if not tenacious about my determination to make a place in Nashville for me and for Becca.

I had signed on for a tour as a background singer and rhythm guitar player. The artist was also a recovering alcoholic and someone I admired deeply. I was one of two females in an outfit of around thirty-five males. The other woman was working crew with her boyfriend, and everyone else had been touring together for years, so I was, once again, the stranger in a group, and I found I could hardly cope.

The artist had made a career recording and was on an arc of critical acclaim and notoriety. We played fantastic venues, along with television shows I had long dreamed of appearing on, but for me, the whole experience was a replay of being an outsider, triggering diffidence and dread. The more afraid I felt, the more I would try to control my situation. I badgered the road manager with an incessant need to know every little detail. I interpreted any interaction that wasn't overtly warm and inclusive as a slight. Becca stayed with one of my neighbors, and I called every night saying I didn't think I could make it another week. The artist told me I was a pain in the ass. The road manager told me I was a pain in the ass. I knew it but I couldn't be otherwise.

I was filling out a resentment list for my fourth step and racking up new resentments daily. As far as I was concerned, everyone was against me. I might have found a way to navigate if I had used the tools that AA offered, but I hadn't bothered to keep a sponsor or get a phone list. And if I couldn't get myself to go to meetings in Nashville, I certainly wasn't going to a meeting in a strange city. When the tour ended, I knew I wouldn't be asked to do anything in the future and that I was effectively fired. I went back to counseling crushed and dug in deeper.

Our therapy group was made up of people whose substance abuses manifested themselves in a variety of ways. In particular there was one man, a successful country music artist who drank once or twice a year. But on those occasions, he drank around and around the clock and all hell broke loose as a result. His behavior was as legendary as his blood alcohol capacity. In therapy, he would sit genially on the couch, an exaggerated smile fixed on his face like his representative, saying little. When he did speak up, he would say that he didn't understand why he was there, why his family, his manager, his record label had insisted on it. He hardly ever drank. Just once in a while to blow off steam—that was it.

He had one of his benders while he was part of the group and wound up in a psychiatric ward. We decided to spend our next session visiting him. He sat on a couch on the other side of security clearance, on the other side of a locked metal door, same smile, same argument. He still couldn't understand what the problem was. Sitting in that unit, all of us trying to reason with him, made it graphically clear to me who my enemy was. The Scripture speaks of the devil roaming the land "like a roaring lion, seeking whom he may devour" (1 Peter 5:8), but his skills become superpowers when viewed up close. He is the whisperer inside us, the inventor of lies, sifting us like wheat and trying to talk us into killing ourselves. Shortly after that, the annual binger quit the group, but a few years later I learned that he had locked himself in the bathroom on a bad bender and drank until he died.

Nowhere were my troubles more acute than in my relationships with men. I say *relationships*, but my encounters didn't really last long enough to warrant that word. My shelf life in romance was roughly around two weeks, mostly due to the fact that I chose men who were unavailable and resistant. I wanted the ones who didn't want me, or didn't want me for long. I wrote songs about my despair over the lack of commitment, the mixed messages, the silent telephone, and I had a wealth of material. When someone came along who was truly interested and ready to pursue me, I wanted nothing to do with him, citing bad chemistry. No kidding. The only chemistry I responded to was bad, and I could locate it anywhere. It occurred to me that this might be pathological. I found a new therapist, this time a woman. I told her my backstory and how I longed to be married, to have a complete family of my own, but I consistently sabotaged myself by choosing unstable men. She said she'd like to be married, too, so she couldn't guarantee that, but after listening to me pour out my woes in the first few sessions, she said it was a pretty safe bet that I needed a lot more than a hug and had my work cut out for me.

I combed back through the events of my childhood and experienced the truth of her prediction. The love and intimacy I yearned for were the things I felt most frightened of and alien to. I had benefitted from some great friendships with men but recognized that when my heart was involved, I operated in pure fantasy, ignoring the distinct signs and signals and reimaging each love interest to fit my unattainable picture.

My career on the other hand continued to gain momentum, a little here, a little there. I met a drummer named Craig Krampf and put together my ideal band with the guitar player I had heard on my first visit to Nashville, Kenny Greenberg, and a bass player named Glenn Worf. My publisher authorized Craig to produce recordings that were artist demos, and my manager, Walt Quinn, started to shop for a record deal.

Becca started school. One of my early publishers, a lovely man named Bob Mackenzie, told me at one point he would like to give me a gift and send Becca to private school. I enrolled her in the school my church had recently instituted. She was a strong-willed live wire, adorable, sidesplitting, and a surprise package of ability. We moved to a neighborhood full of families with similar-aged children. I would glance out the window to see my five-year-old riding by on a borrowed bike, which she had taught herself to ride in less than an hour.

Our landlord, an older man named Mr. Adams, had turned his big rambling house into a duplex, and we rented one side while he stayed in the other. He took an interest in us and became like a grandfather. He favored late-model Cadillacs and had two in his garage. Once he parked one in the driveway with the keys in the ignition, and I spotted Becca in the driver's seat with two younger children by her side, rolling backward, looking determined. I ran outside and stopped the car; she looked at me solemnly and asked how to make it go forward.

I sought parenting help and found it through local programs and from older women who had experience with child rearing. Becca was the central focus of my life, the love that filled my aching heart. I was lonely for a mate and questioned whether that would ever change, but still, I belonged to someone and she belonged to me, and I was deeply grateful for her. When I had surrendered to treatment, I had done it initially for her sake. I had reached the bottom rung of self-loathing where I honestly couldn't say I cared whether I survived or not. But I did care very deeply about her survival. Over time I began to choose life, first for both of us and then for myself.

Slowly I became increasingly comfortable with sobriety. I found that I could still write songs and that my guitar playing improved, but the lyrics were harder to access without the social lubricant that greased the wheels to my stream of conscience. I could get there, but there was work involved, and a cup of tea was not nearly as poetic as a bottle of wine or whiskey. Once in a great while, a lyric would emerge, complete and satisfying, in ten minutes. The rest of the time, I wrote and rewrote and tried to get out of my head and out of my own way so that the effort was not so obvious on the page.

I was not particularly adept socially, but I enjoyed the freedom of leaving any event whenever I wanted or walking away from any person I didn't want to talk to rather than staying and suffering anyone or anything for the sake of the drink or drug. Small talk was beyond me; I did not inherit my parents' talent for party mingling and banter. I loved the deep water of the soul and tended to stay there.

I found that I was able to be present for longer spates without coming completely unglued. I can't say that I found the world a friendly place, and I was ever waiting for the other shoe to drop, but I laughed more and found much pleasure in the day-to-day. But I also realized that I carried a lot of anger and that it leaked. I had made zero progress in developing a thicker skin, and any scratches on my soft spots triggered explosions. I yelled at Becca, my friends, my family, and other drivers using specific sign language. Without the luxury of drinking those emotions into submission, they just flew. I asked God to make me a nicer person. I stuck with therapy. I missed my wine.

Walt took my demos to every major record label in the country and some independents as well. Everybody said *no*, and my rock-and-roll destiny began to pale. In the music business, fortunes often turn on the unexpected dime though, and I was hired to sing a duet with John Hiatt on a Memphis Horns album. The project was mostly instrumental, and the producer was finishing up half of it to send to labels in search of a home. He wanted to add a pop song with potential as a single, and John and I got the call to provide vocals. The recording turned out well and was included in a sample package that started making the rounds. Eventually it landed on Ahmet Ertegun's desk at Atlantic Records. Ahmet was a music-industry legend, the guiding force in many big careers. He listened and said, "Who's the girl?" Shortly after that, I signed my first deal with Atlantic.

My fortunes were changing in romance as well. I met a man at one of my shows who seemed quite taken with me. He had vague aspirations musically, which may have accounted for his enthusiasm. Once we started dating, he maintained a slight distance, like a puff of air, at all times. This was intoxicating to me, and I became the driving, codependent force in keeping what I insisted must be love alive. We had absolutely nothing in common except Southern accents and a love for music, but after we crossed a miraculous six-month mark, I convinced myself that he was the one, that marriage was a given, that I would move out to the country with him, close the distance, and find—at last—true love.

This uneasy alliance continued for another couple of months and then one day he simply disappeared. He didn't call, he didn't pick up the phone, he was gone. When he did finally come around, it was only to say he was moving on. I was beyond devastated. I fell asleep each night in tears and woke up crying all over again. I was convinced that this was my last chance, that there was no one now, nor would there ever be anyone for me due to my disastrous incapacity to make good choices. And I had dragged Becca into this mess too. I had foolishly encouraged her to give her heart, and now she was waking up in tears too. I knew I had to let go, not only of this affair, but also the repeated vain attempts at creating a love story where there wasn't one.

My experience of surrender is not a tidy line in the sand, it is more like: let go, take it back, let go, take it back, let go. The day that I will it and the day that I do it are rarely the same day. It felt like the death of the deepest longings I carried, to be part of a whole, to be cherished and to cherish in return, to have a true companion, bone of bone, flesh of flesh. It felt like a judgment on my substance too. Maybe I just wasn't attractive or lovable. My tendency to ponder things into a powder was not helping me, so I became more tactile in my route to acceptance—I wore Band-Aids over my heart on the surface of my clothes. Everywhere I went, people would surreptitiously point to the Band-Aid, thinking it had landed on the front of my shirt by accident. Or the cashier at the grocery store would say: "Uh, ma'am, did you know you have a Band-Aid on your shirt?"

Each time I would nod and say: "I have a broken heart."

This went on for months. I cried out to the Lord, often alone in my car and thoroughly wretched: "I just want to be picked. I want someone to pick me!" I wept to the Lord, to my friends, my family, store clerks, anyone who would sit still for it. My father sent me money to go shopping, his universal cure. My mother said: "It only takes one," to which I would groan: "That's too many!" My friends said most marriages were bad anyway.

Meanwhile my cousin, my sister, and some of my closest friends had become engaged and set dates, and it seemed that every couple of months, I would be called upon as a bridesmaid or maid of honor. My behavior at these weddings was inexcusable. I was short-tempered and morose, and I bristled at the slightest request for support or assistance. After my sister's wedding I announced that I had retired as an attendant, much to everyone's relief, I'm sure.

But gradually I stopped my sobbing and arrived at a sad peace. I thought of my gratitude for all that I did have, how much I loved Becca and the other people in my life. I thought about the wonder of the fact that I was making a living playing music and was now signed to a storied record label. I wrote more songs, despair and hope in equal measure, and prepared to make my first album, *Big Town*.

CHAPTER NINE

THE ONLY ONE WHO MATTERED

Tennessee

California

As it turns out, my mother was right.

I started recording *Big Town* around the beginning of 1990. Those days were equal parts anxiety and exhilaration for me. It is one thing to dream and fantasize about a cherished notion, but it is something else to live it. I had learned my way around a studio singing on other artists' albums and making my own song demos, but these stakes were very different, and I had received a check for more money than I'd made in the previous ten years. I quit smoking cigarettes to improve my singing. I failed, declared myself a nervous wreck, and bought a carton of Marlboro reds.

I made my first trip to New York and met with my A&R (artist and repertoire) man at Atlantic, Tunc Erim. I met the vice president of the label while I was there and sat in his office playing songs for him. He responded: "As long as you breathe air, we want you making records for Atlantic." "We don't have artists who can just sit down in an office chair and deliver a song like that."

Had I stopped to consider the roster of artists he was referring to, not to mention the content of what was being said, I might have questioned the sincerity of it, but I had waited to hear comments like this for a long time. I had practiced saying them to myself in fact. It was a few years and more than a few hard knocks before I understood that the music business traded on superlatives and hype to keep a full tank of "feel good" at all times.

We logged many days in the studio chasing performances. Don Gant, my first publisher, used to keep a sign on his desk that proclaimed: "It ain't as good as the demo." There is a lot of truth to that comment, and in some instances, we never came close to the magic that was in the first recordings. But with other songs we surpassed the demo handily, and the whole experience of working with Craig and my band, bringing in other gifted musicians and friends whose voices I loved on background vocals, and realizing the vision that I'd carried since I'd first picked up a guitar, added an essential brick to the foundation of my identity. I was a Recording Artist.

I spent days sitting in the control room listening to playbacks loud enough to be heard in the building across the street. I thought about how great the band was. I thought about how great Kenny's guitar playing was. I thought about Kenny. I had known him now for several years, initially as an acquaintance and then later, when he joined the band, as a friend. He was quite the ladies' man when I met him; he always had a girlfriend, and there were usually at least a couple of other women conspicuously buzzing around him at our shows. I nursed an ongoing crush on him, too, but never had the slightest intention of showing my hand, because there was too much at stake. His guitar playing had become essential to me in the way that I heard my own music, and the band itself had an easy chemistry I didn't want threatened. Then, also, there was fear—fear of rejection, fear of scorn, fear of being a fool, free-form undefined *fear*. I told myself it didn't matter anyway, since I had let go and was no longer the captain of my love life. So although I felt a strong attraction, admired his work ethic, laughed at his jokes, and looked forward to being around him, I was sure that any charge in the atmosphere romantically would lead exactly where I'd been before: to disaster.

But something had happened to me unawares while I was sporting those Band-Aids, weeping to store clerks, and trying to accept my condition. I had begun to soften. I had maintained a "tough girl" front in the world to get along, often as one of the guys. I exaggerated those brass tacks, thinking they telegraphed my self-sufficiency and independence. But that was just another way to be at arm's length from people. All those tears had washed off some of that toughness, and in spite of my instinct toward self-protection at all times, I had become more transparent and vulnerable. Kenny noticed.

Over the slow arc of a year, making the record, playing shows and interacting, still as friends, we began to talk more openly, revealing ourselves a little at a time. We found things in common in our histories that created a bond here, a bond there. He would call to confirm a performance date and leave funny messages on my answering machine. I was, in spite of every resolution I had made, responding. But not as I had always done it, jumping in headfirst only to find that the regret far outlived the relationship. I held back, way back, and kept my own counsel for once. I did not consider that I had matured or learned anything in particular. I was simply unwilling to lose the best guitar player I'd ever had over a brief fling. So maybe I had learned something.

Once at a club sound check when Becca was with me, Kenny said he was walking down the street to get something to eat. Becca asked if she could go, and I watched them leave the club holding hands. I thought sadly: *Why can't Becca and I have this?* Another layer of grief rose up and caught me in the eye. I wanted to be in a stable relationship as much as I had ever wanted anything in my life, but I didn't know how. I did know that whatever happened from that point on, I would not be the instigator or the persuader or the flamethrower or catcher. So I sat in the sorrow.

Unbeknownst to me, Becca had been sitting in her own sorrow. She was not prone to many tears and had her own veneer of toughness, discarding the lacy party dresses from Papa as soon as she was old enough to have an opinion for jeans and T-shirts and playing with the boys. One afternoon, out running errands, I heard her begin to cry in the backseat. Alarmed, I asked what was the matter, and she said: "All the kids at school have a dad but me." I had believed that the men in her life—my father, my brother, my brother-in-law, my male friends—were enough to fill the gap left by her own father, but I recognized immediately the fallacy in my thinking. How can you replace a father? She had never said anything about it, but I knew surely there had been questions from other children and constant reminders on any given day that she was missing someone.

I contacted her father that night. As it turns out, he had married, had two children, and gotten into his own recovery program. He was hesitant at first, but after discussing it with his wife, responsive, and we made plans for him to call Becca and then arrange a visit. The phone call went fairly well; I don't think anyone really knew what to do or how to act, so they chatted briefly and said good-bye, each promising to send pictures. Letters were exchanged and a plan was made for a trip to California, where he still lived around the corner from my mother. They met at a restaurant; Becca was shy and fearful, but he and his family were kind and welcoming. From there, the visits progressed, and he made a point of staying in touch.

The funny thing was that once the connection was made, Becca didn't express much interest in pursuing it any further. She went for visits quite willingly, but she never asked to call him and rarely mentioned him. I wondered if too much was lost in the first few years of her life where she had been shaped by my family and my family alone. His ways were not unusual, but they were another kind of normal and not one she understood or related to. He remained, in essence, an acquaintance, and she remained cool toward him.

As the summer of 1990 wound down, Kenny and I made another small turn and began doing things outside of music together. We went to dinner one night, and he talked at length about growing up in a Jewish neighborhood in Cleveland and then relocating to Louisville, Kentucky, in middle school where the Jewish community was small and closed. He described living through a tornado in high school and coming out of the basement with his mom to find they were standing outdoors. On another occasion, we decided to go see a movie that we were both interested in, and a week or so later, another movie. One night, while we were talking, he paused and then said: "I just noticed your hands." My stomach dropped, and I thought: *Oh no*. He said: "They're fantastic." I could hardly understand the feeling of that moment except for this: I was gone.

And so was he. He finally told me late one night that his feelings for me had changed. I didn't know until much later what it took for him to get there. He was someone who kept his life in tidy compartments, and he had an unspoken rule about getting involved with women who were musicians, particularly women he worked with. He was not one to break his own rules, but he said later he reached a point where he couldn't do otherwise. The first time he kissed me was so utterly different from anything I'd ever experienced. It wasn't only lust or excitement, although it was surely both of those things. It was the promise I felt. I knew he was serious and I responded with everything I had.

We were engaged within two weeks. He says he proposed, but he didn't; I did. I had held back for so long I made up for lost time and recovered my old barnstormer style of doing things right now and considering them later.

We had a number of mutual friends who were either amused or horrified. I'm sure not one of them gave us the slightest chance of even getting to the altar, let alone making a real life together. My Christian friends also expressed apprehension, quoting the verse in 2 Corinthians about avoiding being unequally yoked with unbelievers. Kenny had never set foot in a church. He said he remembered seeing me dressed up at a club on a Wednesday night and asking me what the occasion was. I said I'd been to church, and he thought it was a joke because he didn't know anyone who went to church. He was a devout Jew but not a religious Jew. He had a deep affinity for his people, but his experiences in Temple had not been particularly meaningful to him. He said he was drawn to my faith and believed there was a God of some kind, but that was as far as it went.

My parents and my pastor were less vocal about any reservations and more enthusiastic, possibly thinking that this might be my only shot at marriage. My father, devoted to beauty and style, met Kenny, who was wearing a T-shirt with the sleeves torn off, ears double pierced, a lightning bolt tattooed on his shoulder, and half a head of hair, and was polite but decidedly standoffish. My mother met Kenny at my cousin's wedding in North Carolina and liked him immediately, saying he had a strong jaw, which indicated manliness. Becca was cautious at first, remembering, I'm sure, the sad, ill-fated times before, but eventually, just like me, she was all-in.

We set a wedding date for the following spring and began planning a small gathering with immediate family and our closest friends at my mother's house in California. Kenny's parents knew I was a Christian and told Kenny that if there was any talk of

Jesus, they would leave the ceremony, so we had a bit of finessing ahead of us to bring everyone together. We finally found a rabbi, Rabbi Jerry, who was open to blending the two faith traditions and agreed to incorporate Old and New Testament Scripture with psalms. I asked my friend Shawn to sing and also Laurel and Dale, who said they knew a song in Hebrew they thought would satisfy all expectations. We picked out rings in San Francisco, and Kenny, on his own, bought a ring for Becca, too.

I worried that it was all too good to be true. I was equal parts stress and bliss, constantly wondering aloud if we should go through with it, if we were really suited, if the differences in faith were too broad. I spent a lot of time in prayer, asking God if it was okay, telling Him that if it wasn't okay, I'd probably do it anyway. I asked for signs and an answer as clear as an audible voice. I never got that audible voice, but I did know that I was experiencing something real and, in my life, rare—an opportunity to love and be loved. And, if on the surface, Kenny looked reckless and dangerous, underneath there was a steadiness that was sure and devout. He had given his heart and that was it. There was no wavering, that indulgence was mine alone. He responded to my every fit of hysteria with the same certainty: "We belong together; this is right, I know it."

We left for California a few days before the wedding. My parents hosted a party one evening, and Kenny, who was caught in a traffic jam with one of his brothers, was over an hour late showing up. I fell into a panic thinking this was the moment he had come to his senses and realized the foolishness of throwing in his lot with me. I convinced myself he had told his brother to drive in the other direction and to keep driving until he was safely back in Nashville. With a house full of people and without another thought, I walked into the kitchen, which was momentarily empty, opened the refrigerator door, took the first beer I could wrap my hand around—Coors, I think; not my favorite—and drank the whole thing in one gulp. At the time, I was two weeks shy of seven consecutive years of sobriety. Shortly after this, Kenny walked through the door, full of apologies, and I quickly swept this incident into a crawl space in my mind, pretending it had never happened. But it had, and though I did not drink again for some time, I was in relapse.

The festivities continued without incident, and the rehearsal dinner was in Sausalito at the same boutique hotel where my mother had married my stepfather when I was ten and where my sister's future in-laws had hosted her rehearsal dinner a few years previously. I hardly remember the remarks, funny and sentimental. I was thinking about being, at long last, a bride. I was thinking that Becca would have a father. I was thinking that I had a complete family. I was not thinking about that beer.

On April 27, 1991, we exchanged our vows in the living room of the house I'd last lived in with my parents, standing before Rabbi Jerry, who wore flowing white robes and had equally flowing white hair. He looked like Moses just down from the mountain. Kenny's parents beamed during the song sung in Hebrew, and Kenny surprised Becca with her ring in the middle of the ceremony, slipping it on her finger and telling her how happy he was to be her dad. Rabbi Jerry pronounced us man and wife, and Kenny broke the glass. The Jews said: "Mazel tov!" The Gentiles said: "Thank God!" Everyone was elated.

Windsor and her husband, Mitchell, hosted a dinner after the wedding at their house. We left shortly after the cake was cut, spent the night at an inn in Mill Valley, and flew to Hawaii the next day for ten days. My aim in all the planning had been for us to keep the wedding small and the honeymoon big. And we did.

CHAPTER TEN

. . . .

A MOSTLY FUNCTIONING MEMBER OF SOCIETY

Tennessee

Becca and I moved out of the duplex and said good-bye to Mr. Adams, who stood in the driveway doffing his hat and weeping. We relocated less than five miles down the road to a little ranch house that Kenny had bought several years previously and filled with amplifiers and a few odd pieces of contemporary furniture. We were both thirty-four when we married and had talked of having more children right away. We decided to remodel our home by adding a family room and asked my father to draw up the plans. He drove over to see the house for the first time, and when Kenny, after proudly giving him a tour, asked what he thought we should do, my father said: "Sell it."

Ultimately Daddy relented, and I reminded him of his own adage that there were very few houses that couldn't be romanced. He supplied a blueprint for an entry hall and family room along with a master bath, transforming the house into a charming little bungalow we loved.

I had not had anything to drink since what I thought of as "the incident with the beer." We had been given a bottle of champagne on the flight to Waikoloa, but we had passed it on to another passenger, and I looked upon that episode in California as a brief stutter in my sobriety.

Three months later I was pregnant. Kenny told me he had never thought he would have children, that he hadn't thought he wanted them. This surprised me, because he had an obvious easy affinity with them. Marriage and his love for Becca had primed the pump and fully changed his mind though, and he was eager and excited to expand our family. My record label was somewhat less than eager and excited. When I had told them of my impending marriage, they reminded me that I had quite a bit of travel ahead of me and joked that they preferred their artists lonely and available. Later I realized that this was not actually a joke. News of my pregnancy brought few congratulations and a number of questions as to the seriousness of my career commitment. I was in my Wonder Woman phase though, where all the stars had aligned. I had my man; I had my deal; I had a real life; I could absolutely do it all, and reassured them of this over and over.

I went stumping for the record, doing radio tours and interviews. I traveled overseas and visited Holland and Germany. Stateside I made trips anywhere the album was getting airplay. *Big Town* had a lot of critical acclaim; it was one of *Billboard* magazine's top-ten records that year and was selling but not in great numbers. The radio support was spotty and nothing broke through as a single. But for me, it was an auspicious beginning, and the underwhelming response gave me an opportunity to be at home more. There were two songs on the record, "Big Town" and "Walk to the Well," that were distinctly about my experience of faith, and though Atlantic wasn't distributing their recordings in the contemporary Christian music market at that time, I began getting a lot of attention there.

The record wound down, along with my pregnancy, and in April of 1992, we had a son, Henry, who popped out bearing such an uncanny resemblance to his father that Kenny burst into tears. Initially I thought I found my own imprint in his outie belly button, but then it started to recede, and I decided I was merely the host.

Henry was a contented, happy baby. When he first started talking, one of his phrases was "Oh, sure," which sounded like "Oh, shua." Everything sounded like a great idea to him and we adored him.

When the time came to start another album, I mentioned the interest and support I'd gotten for *Big Town* from the Christian record industry to Ahmet and asked him about securing additional distribution there. His terse reply was that Atlantic was not interested in that market and if that was what I wanted to do, I needed to do it elsewhere. He also said he felt I needed to change directions musically and that the next record should be more of a vocal record with an emphasis on rhythm and blues rather than a singer/songwriter effort with an emphasis on rock and roll.

I had been thinking of changing management and was talking to a company that had recently entered into a relationship with RCA and was also a majority shareholder in a Christian label, Reunion Records. They wanted to take me off Atlantic and do a dual record deal with RCA and Reunion, which we did. I wanted

Kenny to produce my second record and began recording *Bus Named Desire* in 1992 with Kenny and Wally Wilson, our friend and Kenny's current production partner.

Making the record was difficult. I was difficult. Kenny and Wally were difficult. They wanted to straighten out my rough edges but rough edges were a big part of my musical identity. The reality was that none of us knew how to enter in this process together. Kenny and I also had no idea how to leave our professional differences in the studio and our personal life at home, so we dragged the whole lot everywhere. At one point, Kenny, Wally, and I went to see a therapist together, and the therapist suggested beginning each day of recording in an isolation booth checking in with one another and establishing a bond of honest discussion. For my part, I would open with: "I hate you both," and then describe my feelings using four-letter words almost exclusively.

For as long as I could remember, music had been the source of my well-being, the place where I had authority and control. All of these years, it had remained my "one thing," and now someone else wanted, in my opinion, to bully their way into my sacred space and rearrange the furniture. Kenny even suggested that maybe he should play my guitar parts. I was inflamed.

Somehow we finished the album, and I found to my surprise that there were things about it I genuinely loved and that others loved too. Once again it made the *Billboard* year-end top ten, and we all learned something about the fine and elusive art of recording. Capturing a performance is, to me, a high-wire act that is equal parts precision and abandon but almost never about perfection in the most literal sense. I often think my part is to invest myself completely and then get out of the way.

Marriage was something of a high-wire act for me too. I loved Kenny with all my heart, and there were peace and joy in the daily rhythms of our life together and our growing family. But, as in the studio, I didn't know anything about how to build a relationship. This required trust, something I was in seriously short supply of. Every time we fought, I would ask him if he wanted to separate. He would look at me utterly confused and say: "What are you talking about?" But I assumed that at the first sign of trouble, you ran. The more deeply we moved into our life together, the more broken I felt.

Becca was struggling too. Kenny had adopted her after we married, and I believed that having him not just as a stepfather but as her legal father would provide the security and confidence she needed moving into early adolescence. It had the opposite effect, however. For the first eight years of her life, I had been her "one thing," her source of well-being. She knew that of all the people in the world, I loved her best and no one else came close. When Kenny and I married, suddenly there was someone else I loved and then, with Henry's arrival just short of a year later, someone else. She didn't know her place anymore and for years bounced wildly from love to hate and back again. She clung to Kenny while doing her level best to push him away, and there were a few epic blow-ups between them. We tried exactly once, when Henry was three, to let her babysit him and returned that afternoon to find him tied to a tree in the backyard.

When *Bus Named Desire* came out in 1993, I found my reception in the contemporary Christian music market was not only less than warm, but in many instances, hostile. I knew nothing of the market itself, of the unspoken but distinct lyric requirements. I was becoming increasingly focused in my desire to follow Christ and wanted to write and sing about my experience of faith. But I wanted to write and sing from that foundation about all of life. There were songs on the record that the Christian booksellers, mostly mom-and-pop stores that carried music as well, declared sensuous and inappropriate. I was newly married and fully in touch with sensuousness. Numerous stores refused to carry the album; Christian radio stations refused to play it, citing no mention of Jesus. The album was popular in the mainstream adult album alternative, or AAA, radio format but was eclectic and probably didn't have any strong singles on it, so I assumed the lack of radio support was justified. But I was completely caught off guard by editorial pieces in a few Christian magazines debating whether an artist like me belonged in Christian music. For the most part, the answer was no, although I had a few outspoken defenders who went out of their way to speak up publicly on my behalf and whom I appreciated deeply. On the pop side, my record had great reviews but, again, not much in the way of commercial success, and at one point, the head of RCA told my management that he was getting out of the "Ashley Cleveland business."

Somewhere in the midst of all these changes, toward the end of nursing and the beginning of the terrible twos, I had a cocktail, and after that, another. I don't remember the day, but I remember how easy it was. I began to tell myself that I had had so much therapy, so much treatment and spiritual formation, surely I could have a drink now and then. Moderation is the pearl of great price to me, the treasure I aspire to but never quite achieve. My friend Rodger talks about how, on the scale of being, he lives and reacts at one or ten, whereas most of life requires that we occupy the spaces between two and nine. I dreamt of navigating two through nine but really only in theory. In reality, that stretch of the continuum was often mundane and, frankly, a bore.

So although I would envision myself having a civilized glass of merlot and then gracefully setting down my glass and reveling in the company I was keeping or my family around me, that's not how it went. When the time actually came, I would stretch one glass to three and then use every bit of willpower I could conjure to force myself to stop. I would do it, but I wouldn't be happy about it, and I would turn my attention to fantasizing about the next encounter. I had no interest in those around me when I was drinking; I was in a private world of obsession.

Kenny began to express his alarm fairly early on. He was not a big drinker and often wouldn't even finish his first glass. I considered him a wet blanket on the subject, and I would argue that I was hardly swinging from the rafters. A glass or two or three of wine, that's it.... What's the problem? He would tell me that it didn't matter how much I drank, that he could see it in my eyes, I wasn't like other people. I would ask: "What other people?" I was surly and defensive every time the subject arose. Then he would walk away from an unfinished beer, and I would empty the can in one swallow before I tossed it. I continued to coach myself that I was just getting the hang of this moderation thing. I would, in time, absolutely be like those other people Kenny was referring to.

We focused on our family life and our careers. We wanted to be together, and we knew we needed help, so we enlisted therapists and also got counseling for Becca. Although my second recording was unremarkable commercially, it sold enough to warrant a third. My management suggested I focus on making an album for the Christian marketplace since I was writing increasingly about my faith. I started to put together a mix of songs for *Lesson of Love* that included arrangements of hymns.

I got pregnant a third time and stopped drinking. Our darling Lily was born at the beginning of 1995. I went into labor while I was recording a vocal and nearly had her on the way to the hospital. We were alive with babies, diapers, adolescence, and music. I can hardly remember those years except that Henry lost a bit of his easygoing outlook with Lily's arrival. He would walk over to me when I was nursing and announce that it was his turn. I reminded him he didn't nurse anymore now that he was a big boy and had his very own cup. He would push Lily's head away, causing her to yelp in protest, shouting: "No, Baby Lily's not hungry!"

I didn't wait to stop nursing before I bought a bottle of wine. I continued to try to strong-arm my way along, forcing myself to quit after two glasses, but increasingly I felt myself slipping. I would plot occasions meant specifically for consumption and express my milk, congratulating myself for being a responsible parent and thinking of the glow that awaited me. On those occasions when I drank without any self-imposed restrictions, I never set my glass down until I was well past the glow, into a blackout, and no longer able to stay on my feet.

My responsibility as a parent became increasingly suspect. I drank too much at a baby shower, of all things, and drove home with Lily in her car seat. I signed on for a tour with the release of *Lesson of Love* with my pal Rich Mullins. I took Henry and Lily with me, three years old and eight months old respectively, and drank my way through sixty-three cities, leaving the kids more and more often to the charge of a nanny. I was full of excuses, but deep down I knew I was in a losing battle, regardless of frequency, regardless of successfully stopping after two glasses (but never one), regardless of whatever I was saying to those around me. I knew. But I didn't want to know. Not yet.

Occasionally I would go into an AA meeting and confess everything. I don't know what I expected; I don't even know what I was looking for, although I suspect condemnation. No one condemned me though. The old-timers at the meeting would simply suggest that I wasn't "sick and tired of being sick and tired." They said: "Keep coming back," and, "Your bottom is wherever you want to stop digging." I thought: *Does anybody say anything other than slogans around here?* I thought those were stupid things to say to someone who was obviously in a tough place and dismissed them all.

I kept my church in the dark, for the most part, as to my struggle, although I'm sure I had more than a few tell-alls in my

Bible studies. I was big on confessing and still awaited the rod of reproof to clunk me on the head. But I felt no condemnation from the Lord or the church either. Every admission of guilt and failure was met with an invitation to come and be a part. I continued to pray and read the Scriptures. Often I would simply hang my head and say: "I don't know how to do any of this. I want to follow Jesus. I want to love my husband and my children well. Truthfully, I just want to get up in the morning and be civil or get through the day with something other than drinking on my mind." Sometimes I would feel the presence of the Lord with me in the room again, like a breath beside me, and I would sense the movement of His Spirit, and I knew He was with me and He loved me. I had trouble receiving such grace. I wanted to deserve it.

All was not sackcloth and ashes though; there were many moments of happiness, romance, and laughter, too. Becca was a live wire and a natural athlete, and we got a thrill out of watching her competing in tumbling and diving. Henry and Lily had their own tumbling style, rolling around like puppies, Henry usually dressed as a Power Ranger, joyous and engaged with every link of ordinary life, strung together like a Cheerio necklace.

Late in 1995, *Lesson of Love* was nominated for a Grammy in the Best Rock Gospel Album category. I could not have been more surprised for numerous reasons. The album had had a larger radio presence than the first two records but certainly nothing of any note. I didn't even know I was a member of NARAS, the voting membership of the Grammy organization, and discovered later that Reunion, my label, had registered me and also submitted *Lesson of Love* for consideration. Finally, this was my attempt at a pop record and didn't have a lot of rock to it, a fact noted by a couple of my fellow nominees.

Having said all that, I was elated. I thought constantly about being a teenager in front of the television, watching the Grammys, and imagining my own acceptance speech. I began working on a new speech, just in case....

CHAPTER ELEVEN

· ·

THE END OF
THE WORLD AS
I KNEW IT, ONE
DAY AT A TIME

Tennessee

My father, upon hearing of my nomination, announced that he would accompany us to the award show in Los Angeles shortly after the first of 1996. I was less than enthused, partly because I was a nervous wreck and didn't want the responsibility of having him along. But truthfully I was more concerned over the fact that he had recently stopped drinking.

My father had a reputation for holding an enormous quantity of alcohol with impunity, but as he aged, he started slipping. My sister and I would hear alarming reports, such as the time he attended a cocktail party, went out on the patio for a cigarette, lost his footing, pitched over a low wall, and rolled down a hill into the woods. He emerged, staggering back up to the house with leaves in his hair and his usually immaculate attire grass-stained, returning to the party, or more accurately, the bar, without comment. He steadfastly refused all offers for rides home, and although he had never been cited for drunk driving, we knew it was a matter of time.

I suggested an intervention that would involve a mediator and an insistence that he go to a treatment facility. I contacted his closest friends to see if they would participate and one of them alerted him to our plans. I was furious at the time, but I think now that perhaps the friend understood something about my father that I had missed. The man wrote to me and said he honestly felt that if we all gathered for a confrontation, my father, whose pride and image were absolutely everything to him, would be so humiliated and exposed he would very likely kill himself.

The outcome of the debacle was that upon learning of our intent to intervene, he simply stopped drinking. I suggested that he might find support and encouragement in AA. He disdained that, saying he had nothing in common with "those people" and that it was all mind over matter and certainly within his sphere to control. He would have been surprised to find that "those people" were some of his more favored friends and acquaintances if he had ever tried a meeting, but who was I to argue? Not only was I not going to any meetings, I was currently drinking, and I really didn't want my father to know about it. But I also had no intention of going to the Grammy Awards without a few cocktails. I spent more than a little time plotting how I would have my way while keeping my father in the dark.

When the time came, though, I was glad to have him along. He had, after all, seeded my career in essence. He had paid my bills when I first moved to Nashville, allowing me to focus on Becca and music exclusively. Except for one notable low point where I was delivering sandwiches for Doc Holiday's catering, often to the very producers I dreamed of working with, I had had the luxury of chasing my aspirations every day without worrying about how

I was going to keep the lights on or put food on the table. I was keenly aware of this, especially in this circumstance that symbolized everything I had hoped for musically. I did note that he was more strikingly turned out than Kenny and I. He wore his beautifully tailored tux. I wore a Betsy Johnson dress that was made for the long lithe body I hoped to find when I looked in a mirror. My own hourglass shape did it no justice, and I could have used a good hairdresser. But my self-consciousness evaporated when we arrived at the Shrine Auditorium the afternoon of the show. I was too excited to care.

The bulk of the Grammy Awards are handed out on the afternoon of the show day in an untelevised ceremony attended by the nominees and their guests. There are celebrity presenters and musical performances, but to me, the thing that makes it magical is sitting in a vast theater among peers from every genre and generation. Seating is open, and I sat within arms' reach of people I knew and people I wanted to know. I was, at that point, sick with certainty that I would lose. Who was I kidding? I had the lowest profile of any of my fellow nominees, and I couldn't imagine that the voting members had the slightest idea who I was.

When my category came up, I shut my eyes and waited for the moment to pass. I had trouble registering when my name was called and just sat there. Finally the presenter said that if I wanted to pick up my award, I better get a move on, and I leapt over the people in my row and charged down the aisle, thinking it would be just my luck to win a Grammy and fail to make it to the stage. It was a rare moment, and I didn't care in the least that no one backstage had any interest in interviewing me or photographing me. Actually I was relieved. I stood in the line of winners in a bubble of well-being, looking forward to a celebratory drink.

After the show, my father fortuitously opted to return to his hotel, leaving Kenny and me to the after parties. And party I did, past the point of celebration, past the point of reason, and straight into remorse the following day. Why had I marred such a meaningful event? What had I said to the people I hoped to impress? I had a lengthy plane ride home to consider my behavior the previous night—what little I knew of it. The plane was full of music-industry people who had been to the awards. Kenny said several of them came over to our seats to congratulate us. I missed all that. I spent the better part of the cross-country flight throwing up in the bathroom. I returned to my seat, stinking and pale, never considering how my husband might be feeling. I chose to accept his silence over my continued excess as tacit approval, or at least acceptance. But it was neither of those things, nor was it indifference. He was well past alarm and moving into fear; fear for me, fear for himself, and fear for our children.

Recovering alcoholics will tell you that AA will sour your drinking. You may return to it again and again, but you return with the knowledge that there is another way to live, that there is, after all, a solution. I carried this knowledge tucked away but never forgotten and pressed on in my quest for normal. Drinking occupied the bulk of my thoughts. It was the first thing I thought of on waking: "I had two glasses of wine yesterday. Will anyone notice if I have three today?" It was the last thing I thought of at night: "I think I'll skip it altogether tomorrow, or maybe just one beer … Yes, just one." In between, my awareness of my thirst lingered on the periphery of the entire day. This preoccupation was a long, long way from normal.

I began to have small encounters with God in my morning devotions. In my efforts to cloak my descent back into my addiction, I would make a show of wholesome activities like prayer and Bible study: five o'clock in the morning., and all is well! I would feel His still, small voice break through my prayers with a simple: "Give Me the drink."

I would immediately commence the same argument with God that I'd had with Kenny: "What are You talking about??? I haven't overdone it lately. I'm not drunk every night. I'm like everybody, anybody. I'm not, I didn't, I'm not …" Somewhere in the midst of all the blathering, I came to a very slight acceptance that I was an alcoholic. But I was an alcoholic who did not want to stop drinking. I didn't even want to entertain thoughts about stopping. I had learned in treatment that the gateway to recovery was willingness—willingness to admit my powerlessness, willingness to admit the unmanageability of my life and circumstances, willingness to surrender to God's care. I needed the will to be willing, and I began to tell the Lord that if He wanted me to turn my wineglass over to Him, He needed to supply me with the will to do it.

Nearly a year passed, and one morning, for no particular reason, I walked into an AA meeting. I hadn't drunk myself into a stupor the previous night, I hadn't been back to jail, I don't remember what prompted me to go, only the ordinariness of the day. Perhaps the recent vacation where my pronounced detachment from my family and desire to be alone with the wine bottle had done it. Perhaps the fact that the liquor-store clerks recognized me now had done it. Perhaps the prayers …

Whatever it was, I went to a women's meeting and told my story. An older lady told me that I should go to forty meetings in forty days. The usual prescription was either thirty in thirty or ninety in ninety, so her admonition stuck in my mind, and inexplicably, I thought: *Okay. I will.* I managed to complete thirty meetings in thirty days and chose a home group to attend. I picked up a silver Desire Chip and made a decisive leap that changed everything. I would follow the suggestions. I would go to meetings, terrified or not. I would get a sponsor and work the steps to the best of my ability. I would lay down my rebel flag and stop arguing. I would take my seat in the group.

And on that ordinary day, I began an extraordinary chapter of my life. I began to recover.

CHAPTER TWELVE

·······················

AFTER THE LOCUSTS

Tennessee

Just before his magnificent prophesy regarding the outpouring of the Holy Spirit on Israel, the prophet Joel tells the people that if they will return to the Lord, the Lord will restore the years that the locusts have eaten (Joel 2:25). In the following verses He says that they will know He is the Lord their God unlike any other and that He is in "the midst of Israel" dealing wondrously with them. Then He says, not once but twice, that they will never be put to shame (Joel 2:26–27). He probably says it twice because shame is entirely destructive and a barrier to the life in the Spirit He has just proclaimed. Or maybe He says it twice because this news is too good to be true for a people who have been behaving badly and He knows they won't believe it because they don't deserve it. But I believe it.

I have seen the Lord rebuild my life through the power of His Spirit on a foundation of honesty and sobriety that is more than I would have dreamed of, let alone had the guts to ask for. But the substance of it is not from a fairy tale; the substance is from being present. I awoke to find my Savior was wooing me with such tenderness and love that I couldn't resist. I awoke to my marriage and found that my husband was ready to jump in and do the heavy lifting (and letting go) that a union of value requires. I awoke to find my children.

Rebecca's struggle to overcome has been a long one. She began a rebellion that was immediately life threatening in eighth grade. The intervening years have included numerous lockdowns, treatment centers, and very bad news. To date she remains on that path, but there is a raw power and beauty in her that belongs to God alone, and I have not lost hope that He will yet claim it for His glory and her destiny. She is meant to be.

Henry and Lily do not remember me as a drinker. They think of Kenny and I as boring parents who get excited over a good night's sleep. When we make vague references to our former wild nights, they roll their eyes and look at us with something like good-natured pity, as if. I cannot even begin to articulate how much this thrills me.

We have had a glorious, steady life together in our family, reveling in the smallest details. The fractured nature of my own family of origin has been absent here, and there is a strong core in each of my two younger children that neither their father nor I possess. All of my children are people that I would want to know and spend time with. And they all are hilarious—which is helpful in navigating the sorrows of this world.

My mother underwent treatment for alcoholism in the same hospital in California where I was treated. She has been sober for many years and attends a meeting nearly every day. She is a woman who dresses up and accessorizes to weed her garden, and no matter how early her AA meeting, she arrives with her face on and her show foot forward. She now lives in the foothills of the Sierras, and I like to think of her elegantly sipping coffee and chatting with the ex-cons and former drug dealers that shuffle into her morning meeting, exhorting and encouraging them to higher ground. They all adore her and so do I.

My stepfather has mellowed over the years, and we have become great friends. He and my mother have had a long, happy marriage, and I deeply appreciate his devotion to her. He is a very good man.

My father developed macular degeneration in both of his eyes late in his seventies. His doctor tried to save the sight in one eye through laser surgery, although he warned my father that there was only a 50/50 chance of success. My father accepted the odds but landed on the losing end. His response to the loss of sight in his second eye was to immediately sign a seven-year lease on a car that he wrecked driving home from the dealership. My sister and I were left with the task of returning the crumpled vehicle to the lot and informing them that they had leased a car to a man who was legally blind.

My father had sold his design firm but stayed on, more or less as a figurehead, albeit one with an active client load despite the macular degeneration. I think his customers, many of whom he had had for decades and through multiple homes, felt that his peripheral vision was better than two good eyes on anyone else. They were probably right about that; he was a brilliant designer. But he was unable to get around on his own, so a friend suggested he take in a boarder who could supply transportation. He had moved to an enormous condominium and the upstairs was entirely unused, so he turned it over to a young bookkeeper named Dustin Neal.

Dustin was single and handsome. He was estranged from his own father and my father took an interest in him. My father had been physically sober for a number of years at that point but had never replaced the alcohol with anything of value. He simply didn't drink. As a result he became meaner and less tolerant over time. He had never been particularly mild in temper or tolerant in the first place, so the result was that even some of his staunchest friends had withdrawn from his life. He and Dustin were both lonely in different ways and found an unlikely friendship with one another. They went to dinner together regularly and took a few short vacations. Dustin was happy to escort my father, and my father was happy to pay the tab. As it turns out, Dustin was a bit more than a freeloader. He had a crooked con-man side that we were all ignorant of at the time, and I discovered later that he had opened a credit card in my father's name and run up a sizable tab. But I knew he was genuinely fond of my father, and my father was equally, if not more, fond of him.

One weekend in the fall of 2001, my father was traveling to High Point, North Carolina, to the furniture market with his friend David, and Dustin told him he was going to a concert in Atlanta, Georgia. Dustin never left Knoxville and instead wound up in a strip bar where he picked up one of the dancers and went back to her apartment. Her boyfriend showed up, killed Dustin, cut him up into pieces, and put him in duffel bags that he dumped on a remote part of Black Mountain in Cumberland County. The police never had a clear motive but suspected what they usually suspect—drugs and money. They showed up at my father's hotel room in North Carolina and, with little or no preamble, tossed him in a squad car and took him to the local station. One of the more clear-thinking detectives realized quickly that the frail man in their custody was in the dark literally and figuratively, and they released him shortly after his arrival. But not before they dropped the bombshell news of Dustin's death, initially and cruelly suggesting my father's culpability. He returned to Knoxville shattered.

I arrived in town late in the afternoon a day or two after he did and took him to dinner at one of his favorite restaurants. His normally well-cultivated reserve was gone; he sat at the table leaving his food untouched and began to cry. He spoke of Dustin: How could anyone do something like this to such a fine young man? He said his love for Dustin wasn't sexual but like a father for a son. He spoke for the first time to me of being gay, of the fact that he would never have chosen it, but that it was just the way it was, and that it wasn't only about the sex but also the companionship and shared interests among his friends. He talked and talked, like a burst dam, tears streaming down his face, and my heart broke for him. I was overwhelmed with compassion for this man who had tried to play the hand he was dealt in the society he had been born into to the best of his ability. Whatever damage he had inflicted—and he certainly had—he had inflicted in ignorance. Maybe it was willful, narcissistic ignorance, but ignorance just the same. The anger I had carried for so long toward him began to evaporate, and I no longer wanted or needed an apology or even an acknowledgement of harm done. I spoke to him about the kindness and compassion of the Lord. He said nothing but continued weeping. My sister and I had prayed for him for many years, that he would find life and peace in faith, but he had maintained his silence in the matter when we asked about it and simultaneously became increasingly sharp and bad-tempered as time went on. Ultimately I found it difficult to drum up much enthusiasm in my prayers for him—forgetting that I only needed a mirror to be reminded that God was the God of lost causes.

Shortly after Dustin's death, the police made an arrest of two suspects, and my father began living for the scales of justice to balance. He was approaching his eightieth birthday and was briefly distracted with plans for an extravagant party. He reveled in the celebration, which was a great success, but fell back into a morose frame of mind afterward, waiting each day for the onset of Dustin's murder trial, which had already been pushed back several times. And then, nearly a year to the day after the homicide, my father woke up one morning, dressed for the office, lay back down on his bed, and died.

When Windsor and I arrived in Knoxville to plan the funeral, we met with the minister from the Presbyterian church. He walked in the door and expressed his condolences, ending with the comment that his sadness over the loss of my father was mitigated by his knowledge that our dad was with the Lord in heaven. My sister and I glanced at one another, and I told him I was glad that he was so confident, but that we, on the other hand, weren't aware of any recent conversion and had no confidence at all regarding my dad's whereabouts. He said he was more than confident, that he was sure because he himself had prayed with him to receive Christ during a visit that occurred shortly before he died. This was stunning news to me, mostly because I couldn't imagine my father praying out loud with anybody about anything, let alone his salvation. But Dr. Barron, the pastor, said he had begun visiting my father regularly when he heard of Dustin's murder and that my father had opened up to him and told him he felt that he had crossed unforgivable lines in the course of his life and he couldn't imagine that God would want anything to do with him. Dr. Barron had responded that he was delighted to tell my father that nothing could be further from the truth, and would he like to be relieved of his burden of guilt? My father responded that he would, and they prayed together. I listened and thought of the kindness of God, to extend peace to my dad, throw him a grand birthday party, and then let him die quietly in his own bed.

My father had expressed disdain for memorial services—"Too maudlin," he said. He preferred a cocktail party with funeral food and much toasting. He would have liked his service though. My mother and my cousin Neel eulogized him with equal parts honor and humor. I did not shed many tears over his death. My grief and loss were in the living years, the silences, the failed attempts to know him and be known by him, and my jealousy that he gave the best of himself to friends, clients, and acquaintances. But I am keenly aware that I, too, caused much pain and suffering for my parents, as well as my own children, and that I have an equal need to forgive and be forgiven. I wish I could have understood this better in my father's lifetime; maybe I could have accepted what he offered without the weight of my expectations that each encounter might be different. But I look forward to an eternity in his company, and I am grateful for my history and that he was my father.

When I first began to play music, underneath the grandiose ideas I entertained, I nursed a hope that I could make a career of it that was lasting. I have released nine albums since then on nearly as many labels. I've taken three trips back to the Grammys and won twice more, once when Grammy and I were simultaneously turning fifty, which was, personally, beyond gratifying. My career bears no resemblance to my original blueprint. I operate off the radar most of the time, in both the Christian and mainstream marketplaces, but I belong to neither and am largely unknown as an artist. Yet I have had a remarkable career that has taken its own unlikely course down into the trenches of everyday life where I have gotten to know my audience, often on a first-name basis.

I have interacted with many of the best musicians from nearly every genre and have found a true community in Nashville, right in the heart of my beloved native Tennessee. I am free to sing what I want, write what I want, and play where I want. There are times when I have dishonored the gift I've been given. I have reacted to disappointment by withdrawing and declaring that I would rather do the dishes than play music. The business can be a cruel one; I have yet to meet an artist who didn't take it all personally. But eventually I have returned each time to my first love, sitting down with a guitar in a room by myself and making something out of nothing.

My lack of commercial success has been a great gift to my children. I'd like to say that I took less of a career for their sakes, but truly it's just the way things turned out. I had enough demand to stay in the game but no more, and the result is that I've been consistently present and engaged in every aspect of their lives. I made many, many mistakes with all of them, particularly Rebecca, who received the brunt of my alcoholic insanity. But as my recovery, and the peace that accompanies it, deepened, I was able to be the mother I had hoped to be, and as time went by, I realized that, as usual, I had been gazing west looking for fulfillment when I should have been looking east, because all the success in the world does not compare to loving well and receiving love. It is the thing we were made for.

The first thing that I fell in love with in Kenny was the way he played his guitar. I have never gotten over that. He has a way of saying the things that have no words through playing. He has followed through in that unspoken language in our marriage, expressing his devotion to me and to our children in innumerable ways. When we first married, I devoted much prayer to asking the Lord about his salvation. When would he come to Jesus? What could I do to move things along? Each time I sensed the same admonition: "Mind your own business and trust Me." This is one of my least-favorite activities. I should have been relieved; I had more than enough to deal with in regard to my own spiritual condition, which often felt tenuous at best. But I worried and fretted and lamented the fact that trust was not something I had a lot of experience with. I dragged Kenny to church, and on more than one occasion lectured him like a schoolmarm on his need for the gospel. But as my own issues surrounding life and faith brought increasing struggle and preoccupation, I ultimately left him to God. As it turns out, he was in very good hands. Kenny was baptized ten years ago in the Frio River at Laity Lodge, our favorite place in the Texas Hill Country. We marvel at our many years together. How can it be? One day and then another.

In *Life Together*, Dietrich Bonhoeffer wrote: "Every day is a completed whole. The present day should be the boundary of our care and striving. It is long enough for us to find God or lose God, to keep the faith or fall into sin and shame. God created day and night so that we might not wander boundlessly, but already in the morning may see the goal of the evening before us."[4] It has not been easy for me to stay put in the day; I personally would like a detailed outline for the next twenty years. There are days that I don't want to end, and days that I can't put behind me fast enough, but I know that whatever is in front of me is reality; and if it's joyous reality, I want to savor it; if it's painful reality, I can, by grace, endure it; if it's ordinary reality, I want to feel the comfortable rhythm of it. All of these can and should be done twenty-four hours at a time.

CHAPTER THIRTEEN

MORE BROKEN, MORE LIGHT

Tennessee

I remember reading in the AA *Twelve Steps and Twelve Traditions* that in recovery we have an opportunity to exchange our selfishness and isolation for friendship and service: "A friend among friends and a worker among workers." I initially likened that description to a green participation ribbon meaning *nobody special* and thought to myself: *Who wants that?* Over the years I have found that what that sentence is referring to is getting right-sized—not too grand, not too small, and simply belonging to the whole. Belonging. I have emerged from my own isolation to find that I love belonging, to the body of Christ, to the program of AA, to the human community. I have been invited in from the margins, not as a guest artist but as a family member.

Still I have many days where I lead with arrogance and default to a cold spot of indifference. I have a far greater understanding of humiliation than I do of humility, and on the rare occasions that I do yield to humble service, I look for opportunities to point it out in a large group setting. To that end, I have tools now that help me stay, as they say, between the ditches.

I am, by nature, a ridiculously early riser. I love the quiet and solitude of the morning and the emerging light that reminds me of the new mercy of each day. I generally have a devotional, which can be brief or lengthy but that includes prayer that God would create a clean heart in me, fill me with His Spirit, and use me somewhere in His plans. The writer of the book of Hebrews declares that the Scriptures are a living document that reveal the thoughts and intent of the heart (Heb. 4:12). I know this to be true and return to them daily to study, to try to walk out, and more recently, to teach. I do not kid myself that I have any big corner on illumination, and I feel the weight of the mystery often. But I do trust that God will give me the understanding I need on any given day to stumble forward into His marvelous light and to avoid the "innovations in dogma" that Scott Cairns refers to in his poem "Doctrinal Treatises."

I started memorizing Bible passages a few years ago, initially just to see if I could, and then to fill my head with a voice other than mine. I found the same lamp that King David describes in Psalm 119, saying that he takes heed to God's word, keeps it, hides it in his heart, remembers it, meditates on it, is revived by it, strengthened by it, led by it, hopes in it, trusts in it, and lives. Me, too.

In AA, recovery is found in the twelve steps, which are often compared to the beatitudes and deeply effective in balancing my life. We often say in meetings that it's too bad that everyone isn't eligible for this program, because they are missing an opportunity to live within a structure that provides maximum benefits. I am nearly always in these steps; I've worked them formally and in order several times and continue with the last three of them almost daily. In *Power to Choose*, Mike O'Neil defines the steps as making peace with God, with others, and with ourselves. We then simultaneously keep that peace and pass it on. The first three steps are about recognizing that only a spiritual solution will save me from alcoholism and yielding to a power greater than myself to provide sanity and sobriety. Steps four through ten have to do with taking a look at my behavior, my offenses and resentments, past and ongoing. I acknowledge them, confess them, make amends, and continue to make an effort to address my character defects and to keep a spiritually clean house. The eleventh step is about developing my relationship with God through time spent in His presence, and the twelfth step is about passing on the gift of sobriety that I've been given by carrying the message to other alcoholics. In a fundamental way, these steps have put feet on my faith and provided a framework for living and living well.

There is a movie called *The Kid* where Russ, a self-involved, tightly wound, generally unpleasant man, awakes one morning to discover a younger, chubby version of himself named Rusty watching TV in his chrome-and-leather living room. Rusty's role is to get Russ back in touch with his lost humanity, a task that is not easily accomplished, and at one point in the movie, Rusty becomes so exasperated that he shouts at Russ: "You are such a loser, you don't even have a dog!" The events of my childhood surrounding pets were sufficiently heartbreaking to keep that door closed well into my adulthood. When I did bring a dog into the household, I kept my distance and, as dog lovers know, distance does not work with canines. But as I "came to" in my life, I realized at one point that animals added a dimension that humans could not supply. I returned home from a particularly intense and valuable experience of therapy at a place called OnSite and announced to Kenny and the kids that I was getting a dog. Since then I've brought three puppies into our home and hearts, throwing myself into training and folding them into the constancy of our lives. I have given my whole self to these pets, and they have given their whole selves to me. I have also had to let go, one to cancer and one to sudden death that I was unprepared for and nearly bedridden over, but even then, I would not have missed the joy of having them. As I write, my little dog Samson is draped across the back of the couch nearby and that companionship is a rich source of contentedness and healing. I intend to be in the company of dogs for the rest of my life.

One of my dogs, King Curtis, was a big German shepherd with an insatiably high drive. Without exhaustive exercise, he would pace the house, waiting for an assignment. As soon as he was old enough, we began hiking in a nearby park, and over the course of his life, we logged mile after mile at all hours, in all weather, day after day. I credit him for opening the activity door wide in my middle age. I cannot say that I initially loved exercise. I did it for sanity—his and mine. But over time, I came to depend on it as much as he did. The first year that I had him I lost twenty-two pounds, and from there, went on to become a runner, starting with what can only be described as plodding for a half a mile to a regular weekly course of sixteen to twenty miles. There are many mornings that I do not feel like putting on my running shoes, but I'm always better for it, and during one period when I was sidelined with an injury, I was surprised at how much I missed it. I would gaze at other runners with the same longing that I reserve for ice cream and cake.

I also cannot say that my issues with food are entirely resolved. Most of the time I am at peace with eating moderately and turn my attention to other things to fill my life. But sooner or later I return to it with a devotion that is nothing short of idolatrous. On occasion, I'll sit down with something as pedestrian as an unopened box of cereal, and I won't stand up until it's empty. I have made much progress from the days when I would literally wreck my car reaching for a bucket of Kentucky Fried Chicken, but for now, food obsession provides a regular reminder that I am still an addict.

My friend Mike was lamenting this lack of power once, commenting that we should be walking on water, just like Jesus. Another friend, my AA sponsor Pam, who had a hemorrhagic stroke at the age of sixty and is fighting daily to regain the use of her left side, said she'd be happy to walk at all. This is the miracle: that I walk at all. I am deeply grateful for every day that I can get out of bed in the morning and return to it at night without a drink.

Years ago I picked up the Life section of the Sunday paper and read an article about a woman named Aolar Hart who had turned her restaurant into a homeless ministry called God Almighty, as per the Lord's instructions. She said everyone was welcome, and she was ready to serve them biscuits and the Bible. She said she didn't let anyone wallow drunk in her place, but she never sent them out the door without a sandwich and a hug. The writer from the paper commented that nearly the whole neighborhood called her *Mama*, and people with no place else to go found refuge and a meal with Pastor Hart. One person, a transgender named Tamika, showed up, and though Pastor Hart was initially taken aback, she quickly admonished herself: "Saint Peter, just hush up and open those gates. God loves everybody." Then she went home to her own closet and got him a dress.

I found myself in tears reading this story. It reminded me of my own encounter with Jesus and a passage in one of my favorite books: *Salvation on Sand Mountain*. The author, Dennis Covington, describes the way his father summoned him to supper in the evenings saying: "He always came to the place I was before he called my name." I thought of all the times I had felt the presence of my heavenly Father in the place I was, requiring nothing, surrounding me with love.

I got in my car and drove into the inner city to God Almighty and met Pastor Hart. I told her how moved I was by her love for Tamika and her simple act of acceptance in giving her a dress. She interrupted me and said: "Oh no, honey, not just a dress. Oh no, it was my best dress—otherwise, what's the point?" I told her I wanted to be of service to her. She said: "Well, that's great. I've got to run some errands; I'll be back in a few hours, feed the people."

I said: "You're not going to leave me here by myself, are you?"

She said: "Oh, you'll be fine. Here's bread; here's bologna; here's hot sauce. Make them a sandwich and give them a hug."

Thus began a great friendship and a lesson in loving others. I want to love and serve those whom God leads me to without qualification. Sometimes I serve with enthusiasm, other times complaining and resisting, but how can I refuse the One who has given me everything? And truly, if I don't give myself away, I'm stuck with myself.

I had a pastor for many years who forbade us to sing "I Surrender All," because he said it was a crock. He said no one surrenders all and that most people, if they are honest, aren't even qualified to sing "I Surrender Some." I am solidly in that camp. I know all about selective surrender and cherry-picking my life before handing it over to God's care: "Here, You can have this. I didn't want it anyway." God knows all about it too, but here's the thing: a little bit of surrender is a lot of surrender. By the same token, a little bit of hope is a lot of hope. A little bit of faith is a lot of faith. All of these things have the same source: a heavenly Father who is so entirely counterintuitive that He delights in investing His power in tiny things like mustard seeds and broken fools like me. I don't really foresee a day when I will let go without a fight, but it's helpful to remember that I am not, as Richard Rohr says, "giving up but giving to." There is an enormous difference.

One Sunday at my church, I watched an acolyte with a tall staff topped by an ornate cross lead the children down the aisle before Communion to return from Sunday school to their families. Most of the children just tumbled along, scanning the pews for their parents, but one little boy was just a step or two behind the acolyte, gazing up, fixed upon the staff. I watched the procession as we all sang: "Lamb of God who takes away the sins of the world, have mercy on us," and recognized something of myself in the boy. I am following that cross as closely as I am able. Not in triumph—though I still ask God regularly if I can take a victory lap as the hero—but as a beggar who has found the path of life. I am ever reminded that I am the little black sheep who was rescued by the One who is the Shepherd and the Lamb of God; the Redeemer who lived in human frailty and easily inhabits mine. To live is Christ; to love is Christ. Christ is all and in all.

NOTES

[1] Ashley Cleveland, "Little Black Sheep" © 2012 Sole Sister Music (BMI), administered by Bug Music.

[2] Alcoholics Anonymous World Services, Inc., *The Big Book*, fourth edition (Alcoholics Anonymous, 2001), 83.

[3] Ashley Cleveland and Madeline Stone, "Broken Places," *Second Skin* © 2002 Sole Sister Music (BMI) and Stonesville Music (BMI).

[4] Dietrich Bonhoeffer, *Life Together* (New York: Harper & Row Publishers, 1954).

VISIT ASHLEY AT HER WEBSITE:
ASHLEYCLEVELAND.COM,
OR ON TWITTER:
TWITTER.COM/ASHLEYCLEVELAND
· ·

FIND THE SONG
"LITTLE BLACK SHEEP"
BY ASHLEY CLEVELAND
ON ITUNES.
AVAILABLE FOR DOWNLOAD SEPTEMBER 1.
· ·

TO FIND OUT MORE ABOUT THE COVER
ARTIST, VISIT DLTAYLORARTWORK.COM
· ·